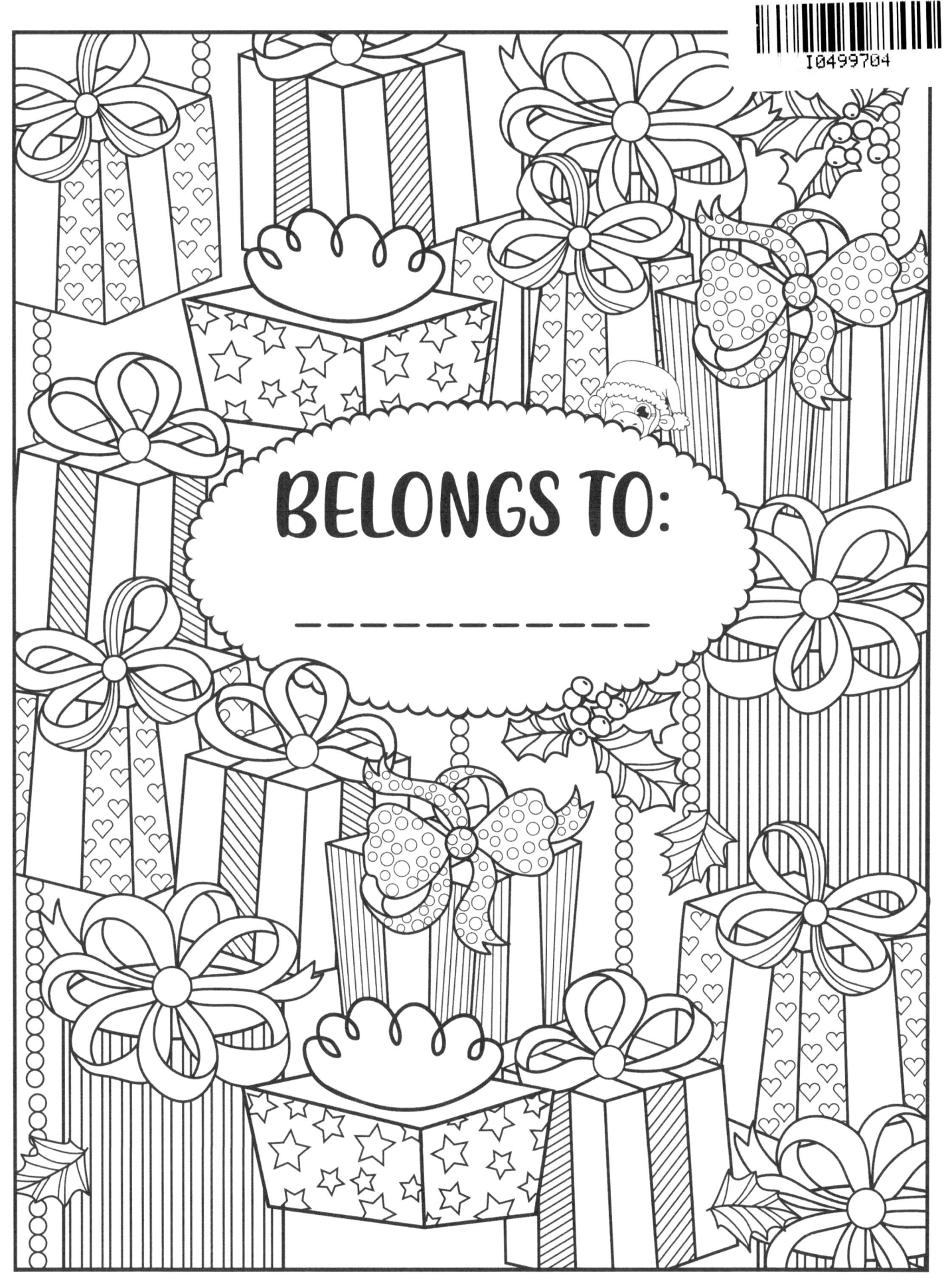

BELONGS TO:

_____

COLOR TEST PAGE

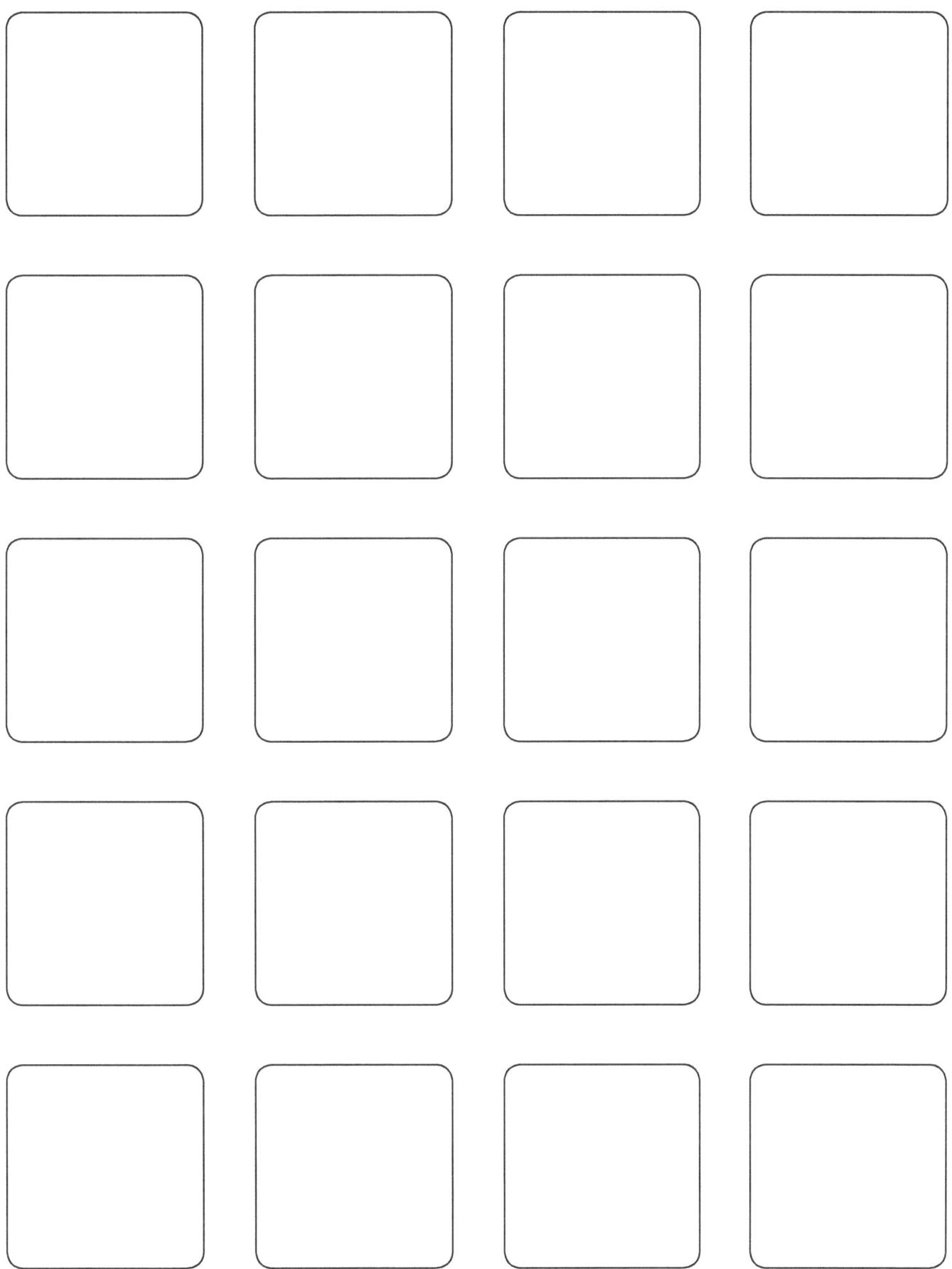

SNOWMAN

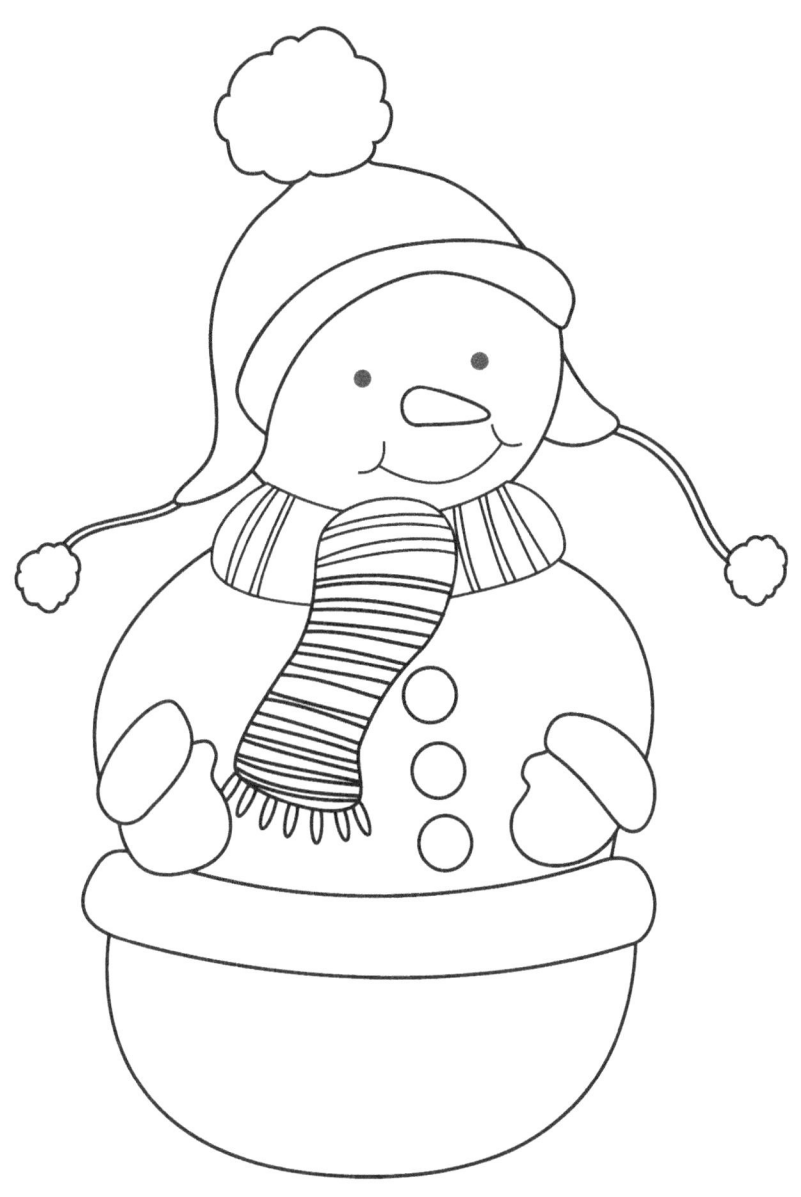

SNOWMAN

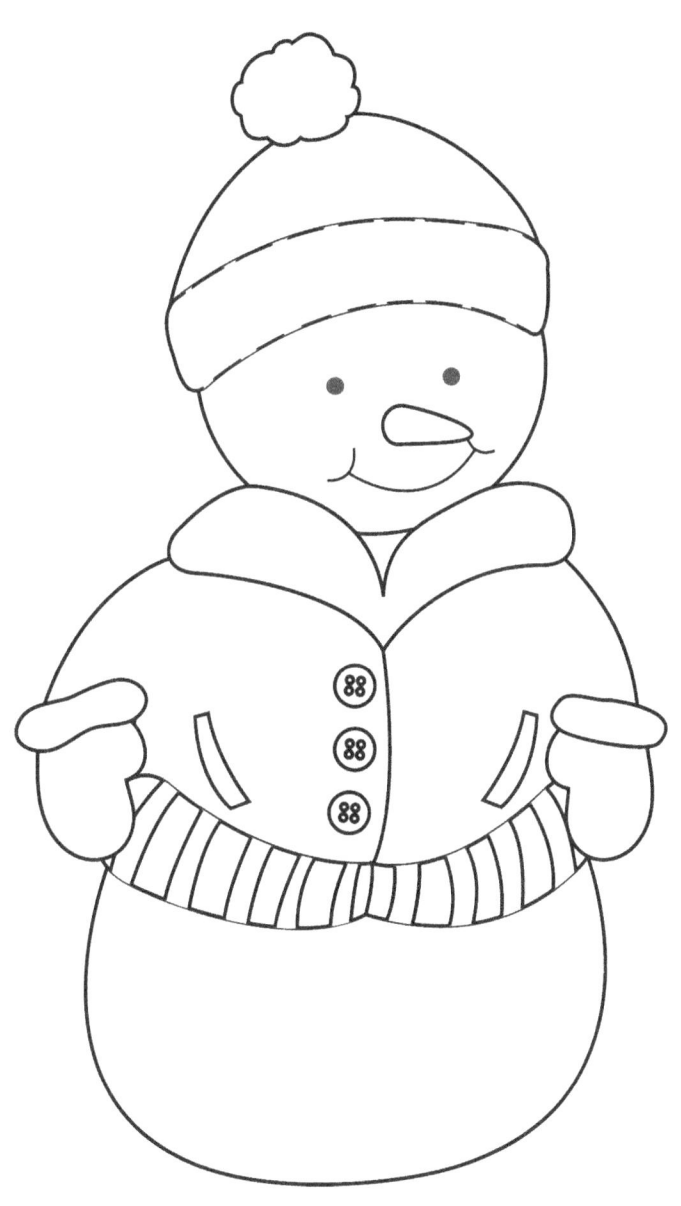

SNOWMAN

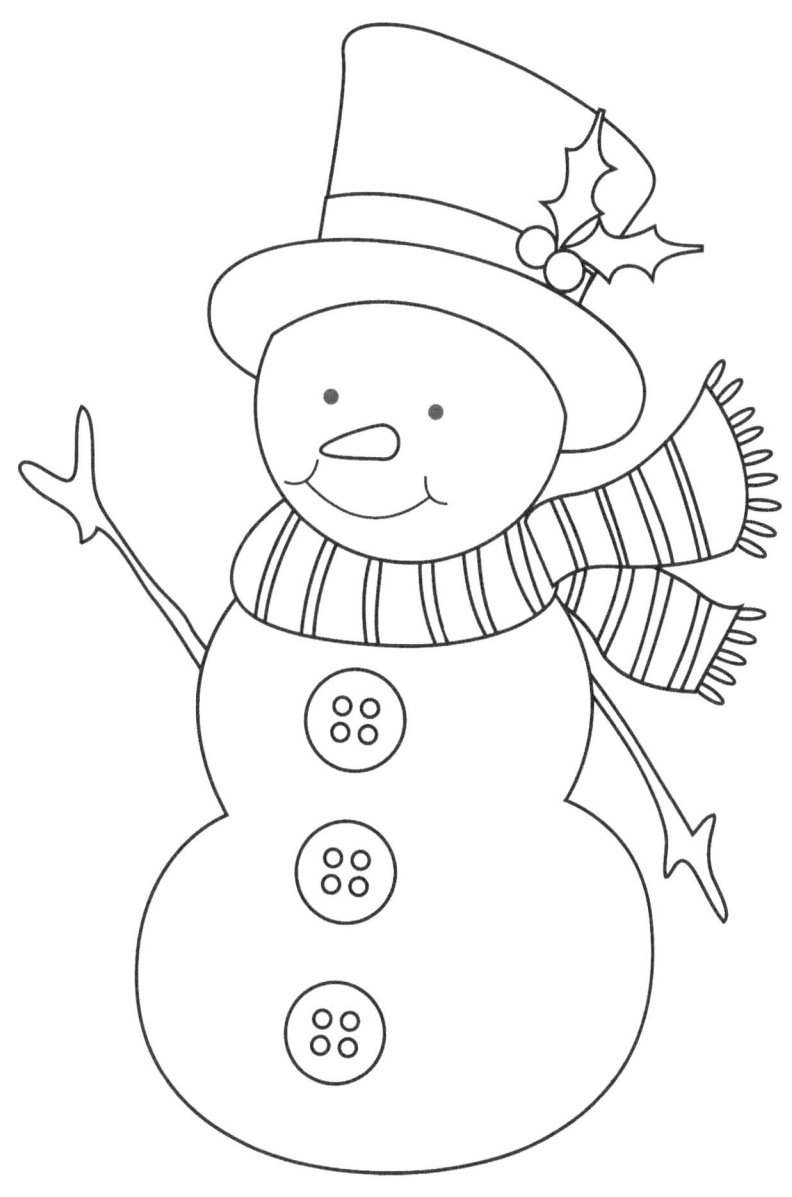

SNOWMAN

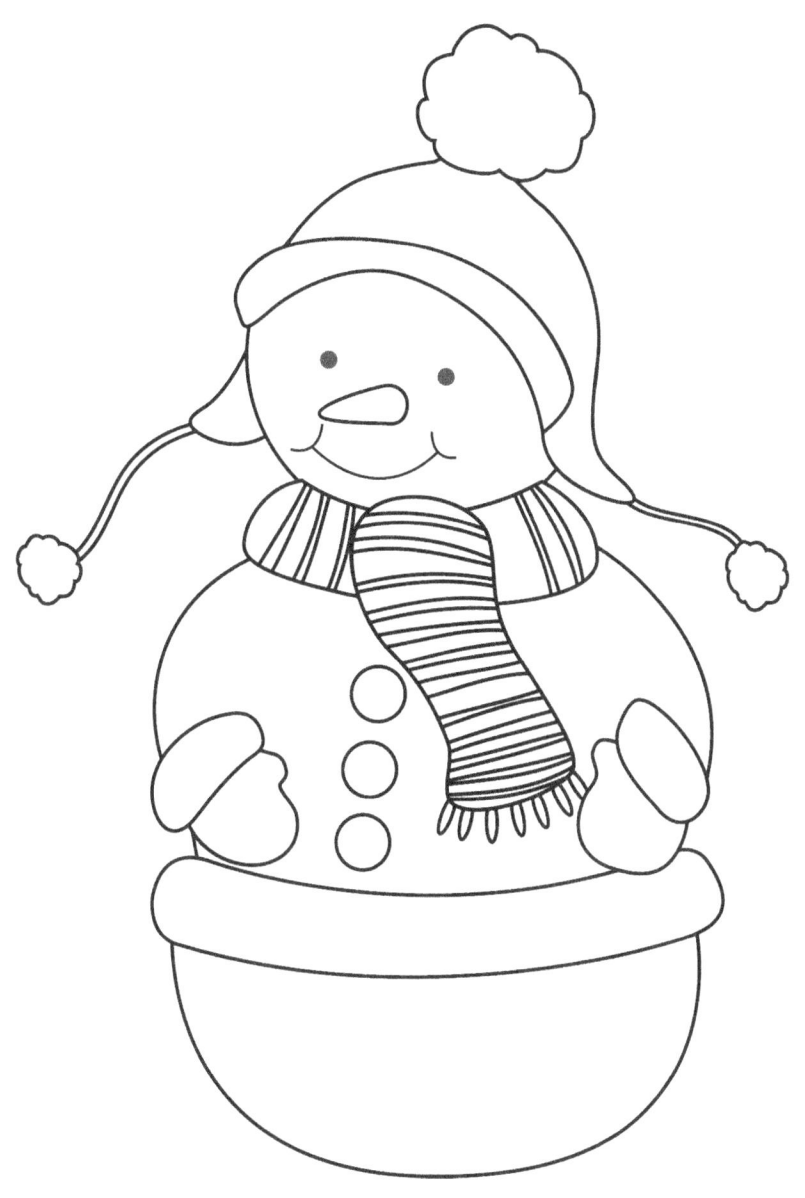

SNOWMAN

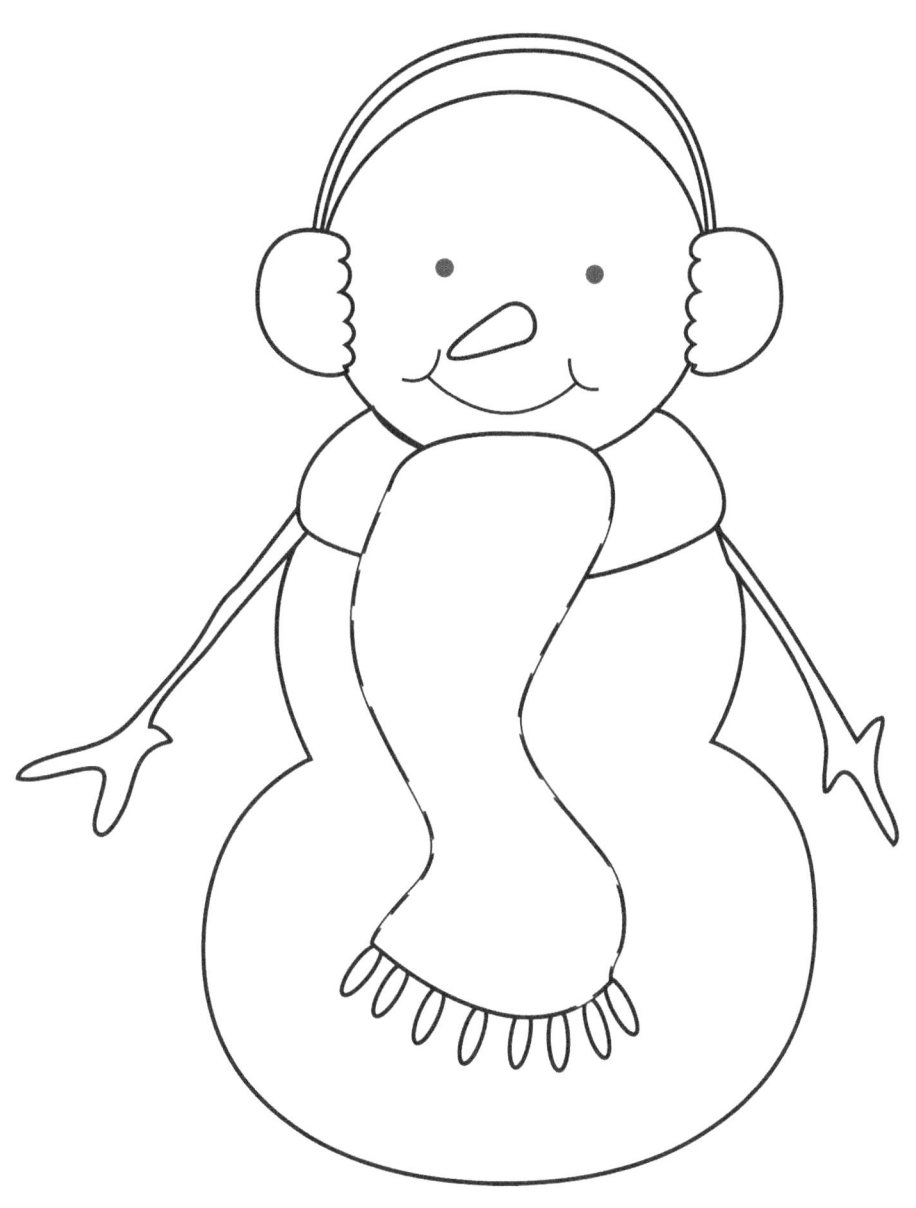

GINGERBREAD

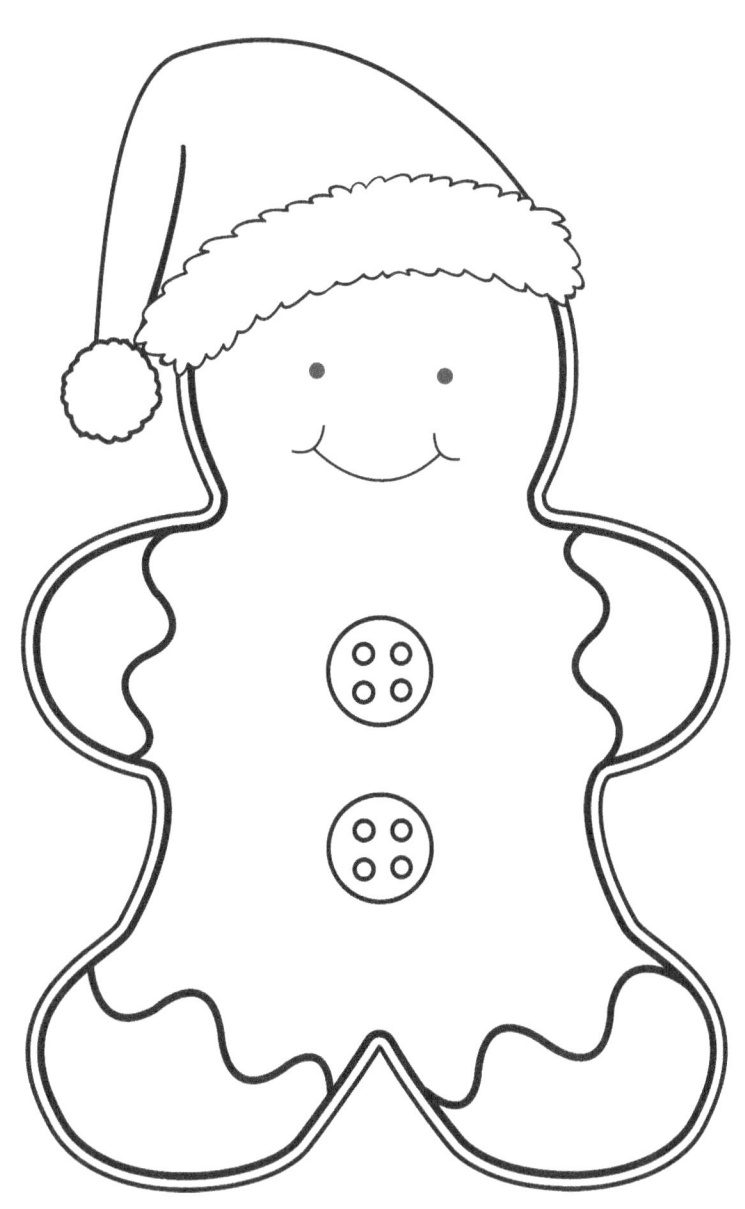

GINGERBREAD

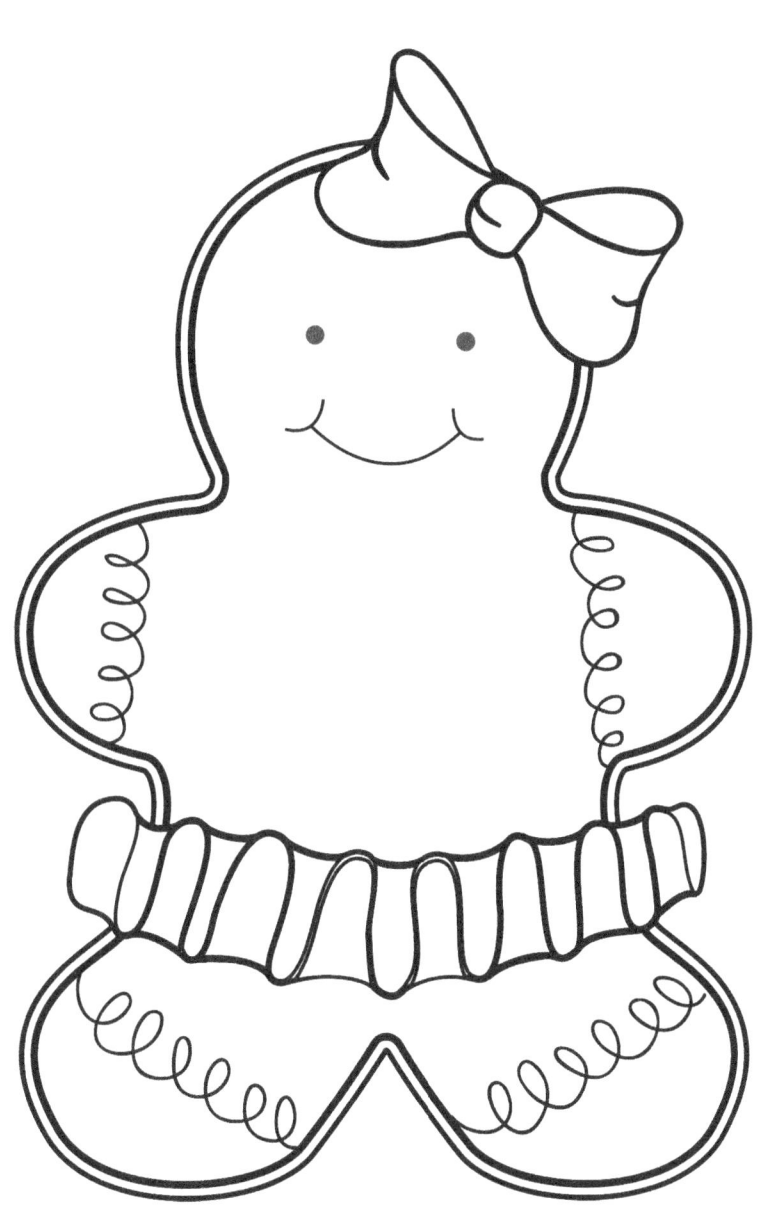

GINGERBREAD

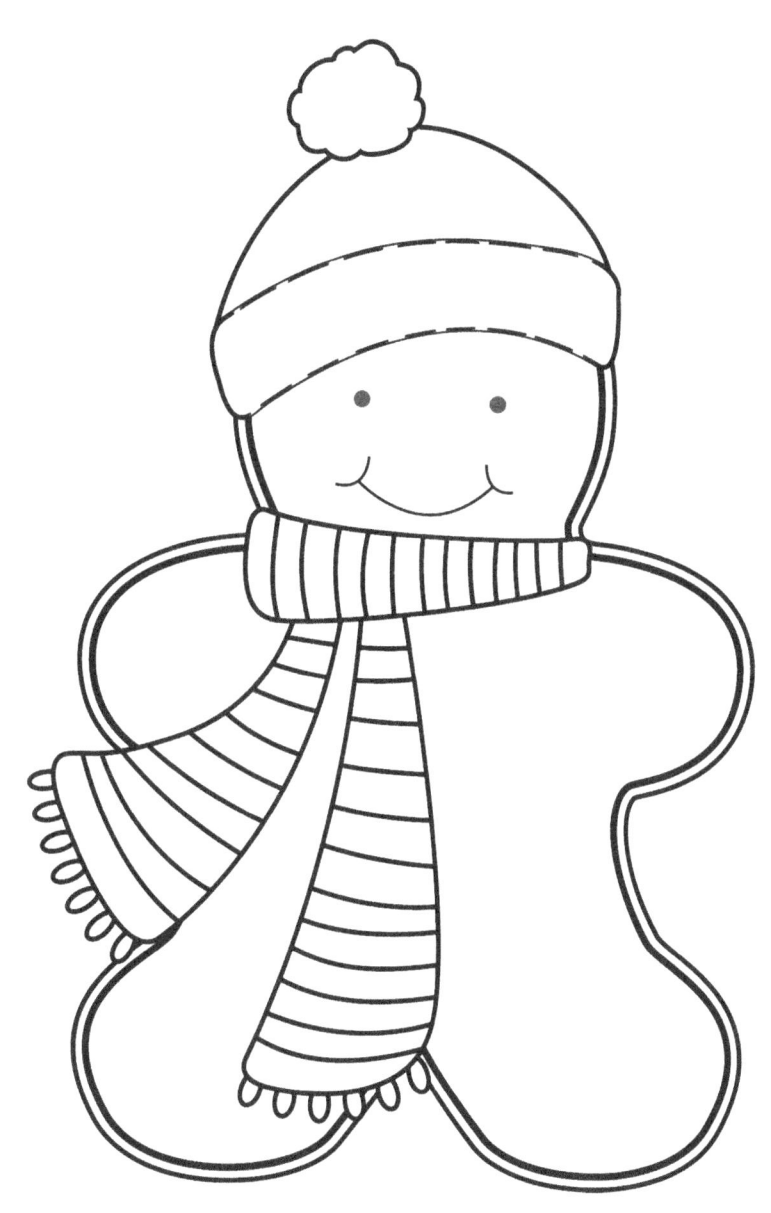

GINGERBREAD

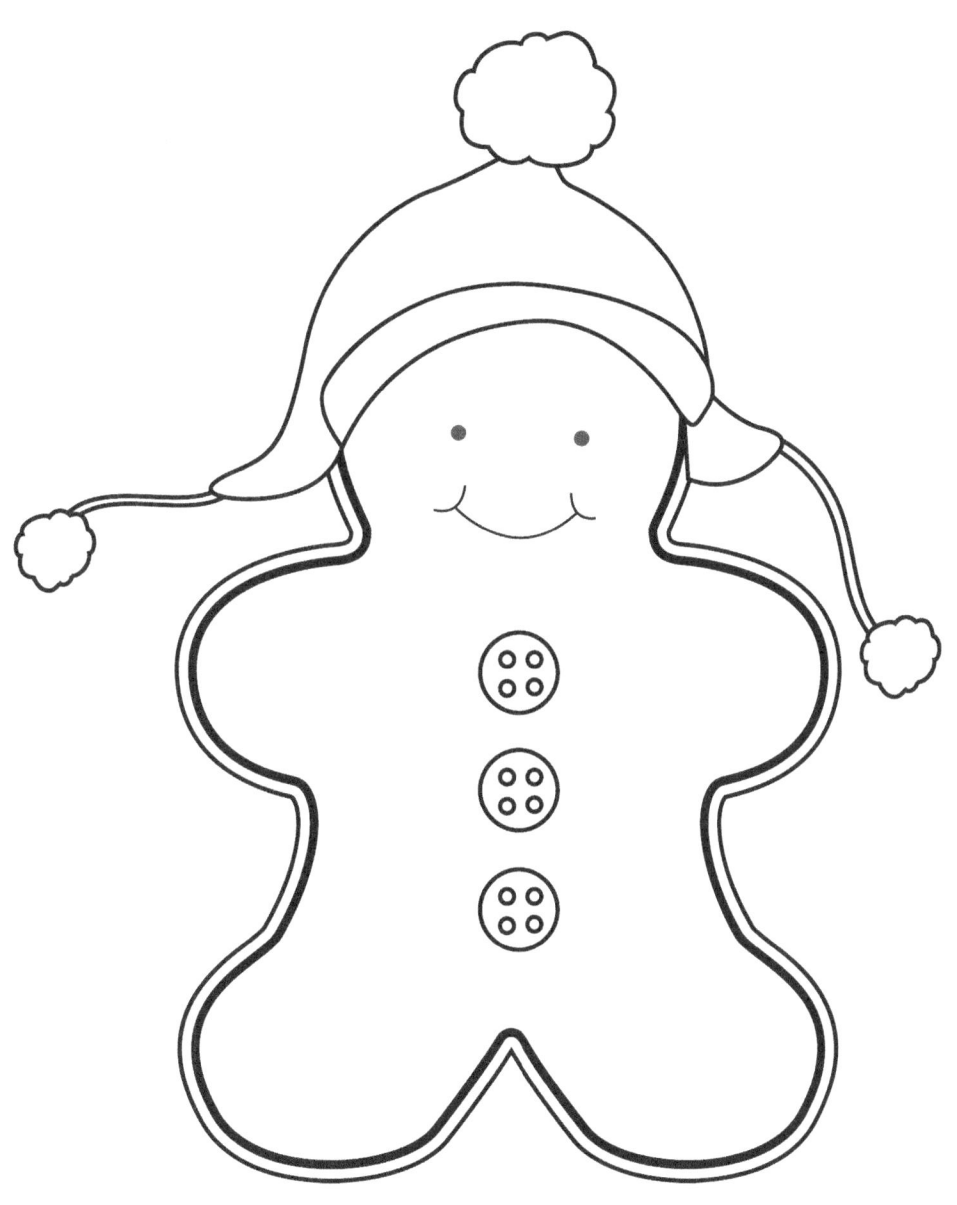

GINGERBREAD

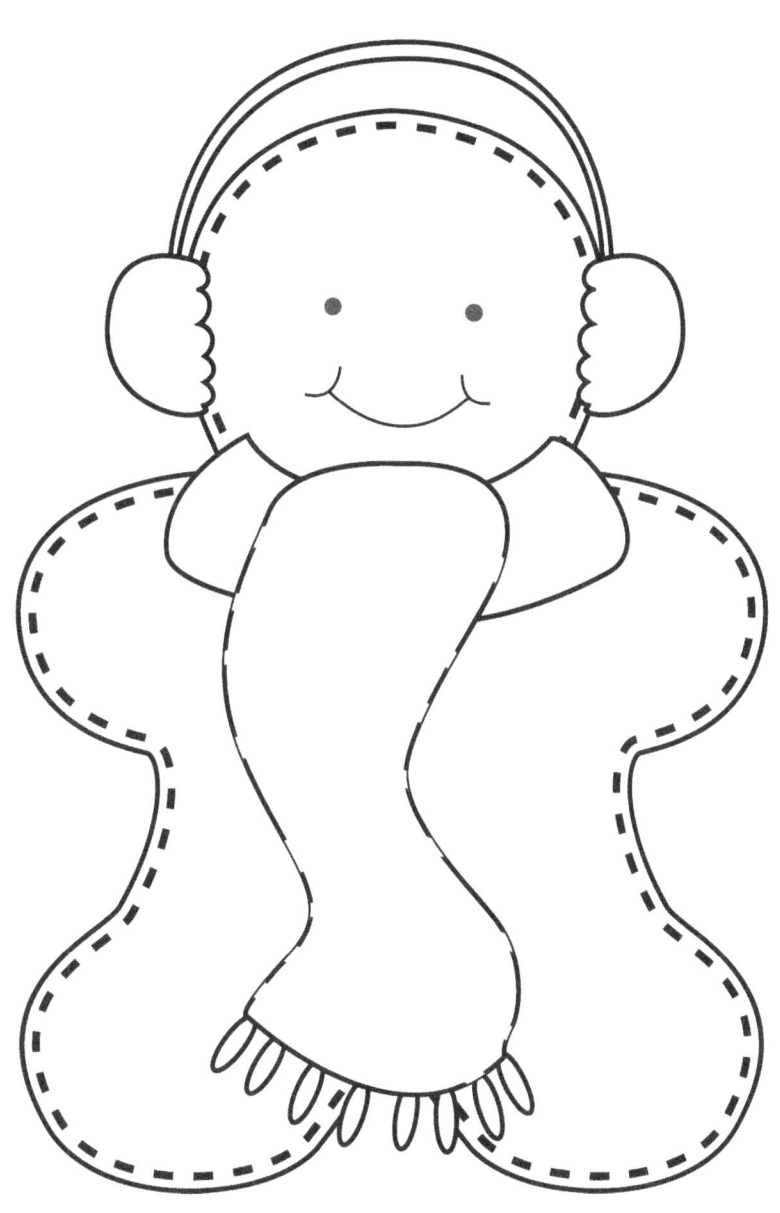

ELVES

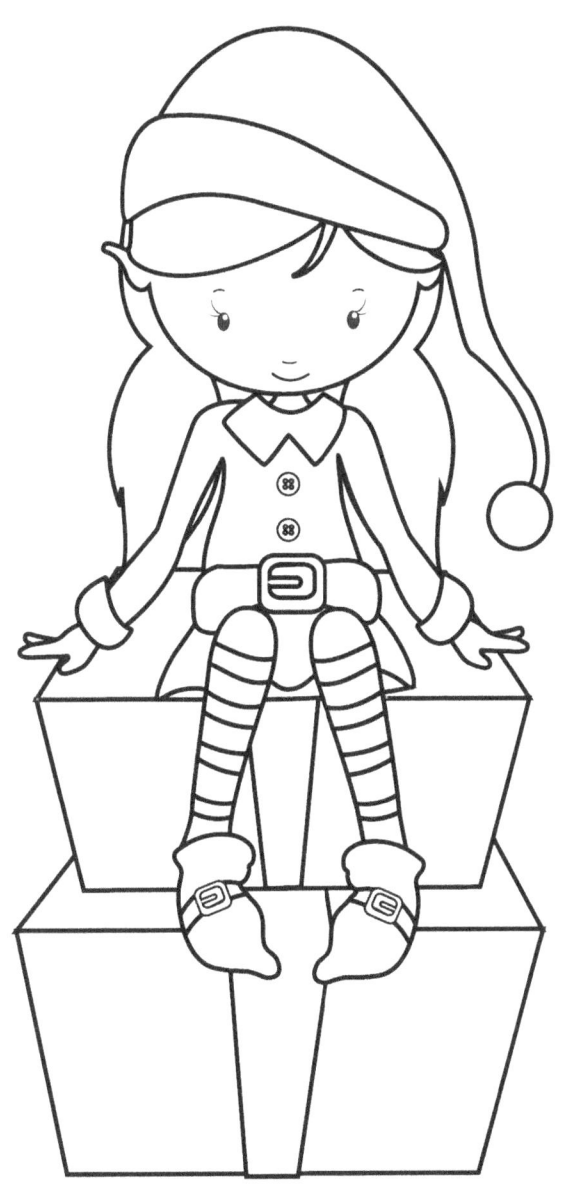

ELVES

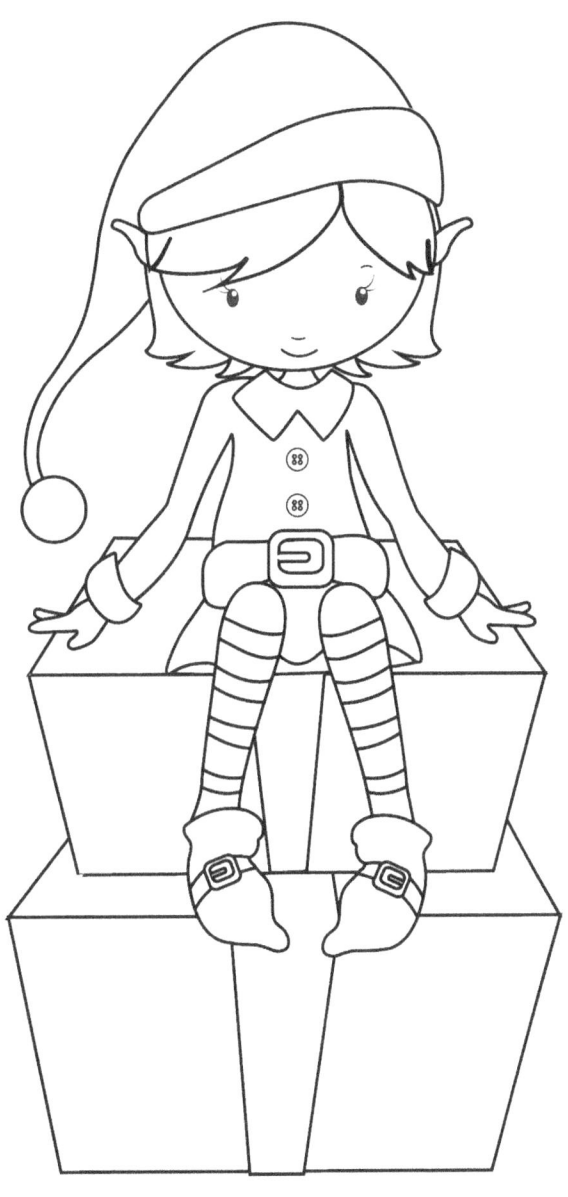

ELVES

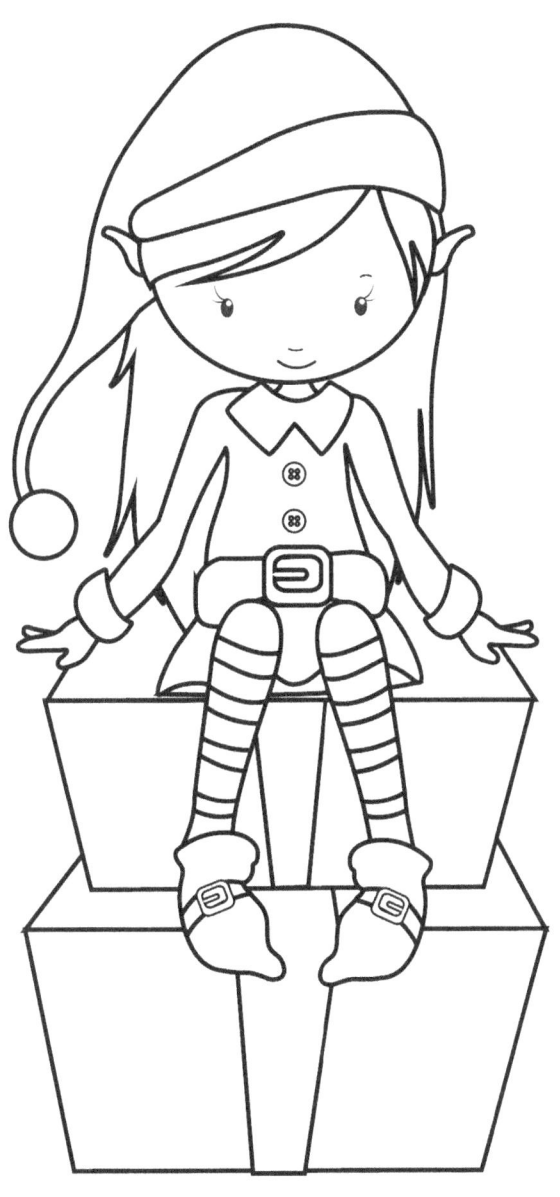

ELVES

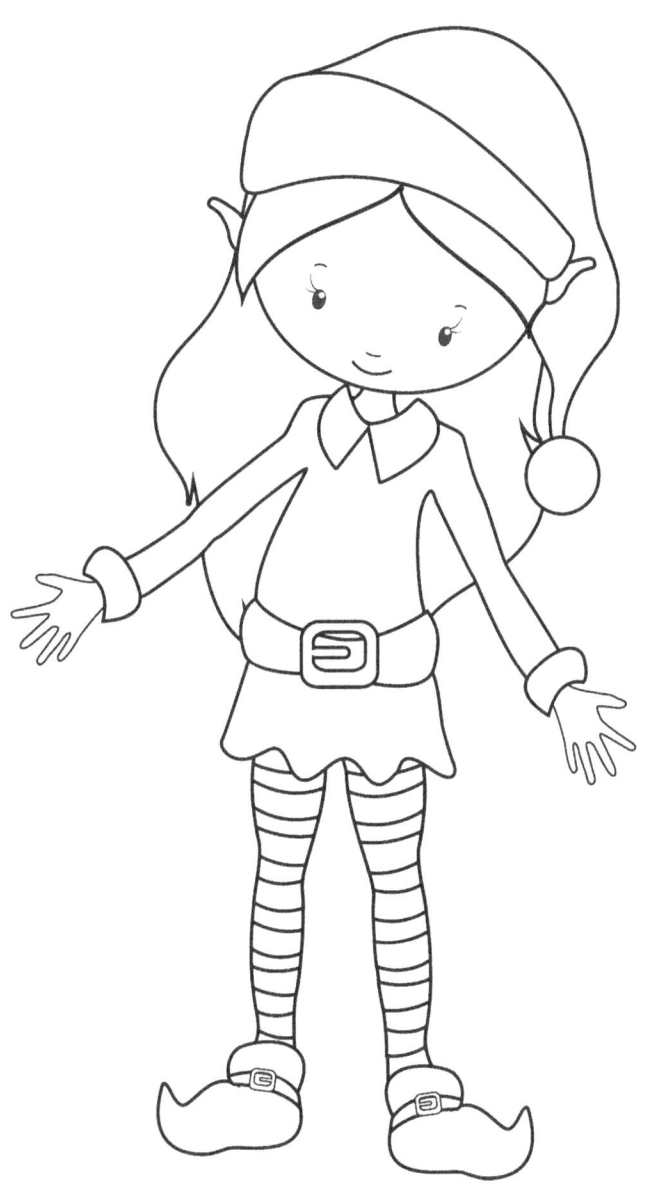

ELVES

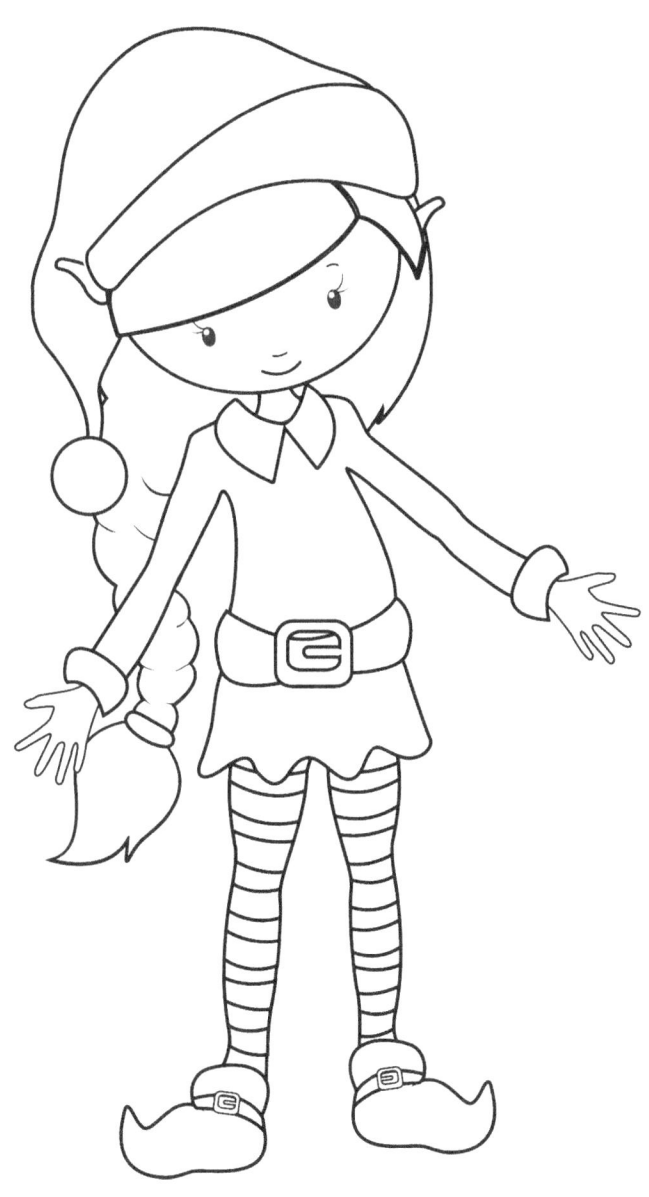

WOODLAND

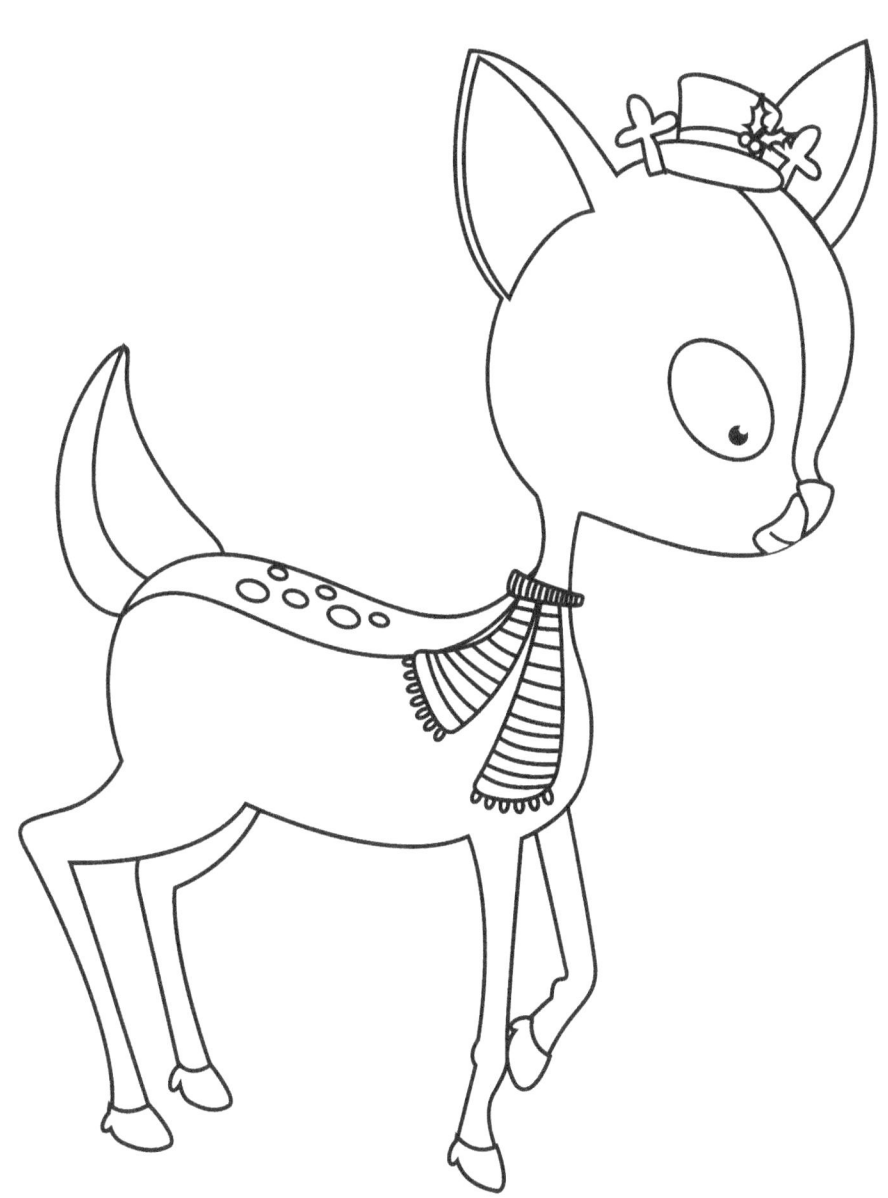

WOODLAND

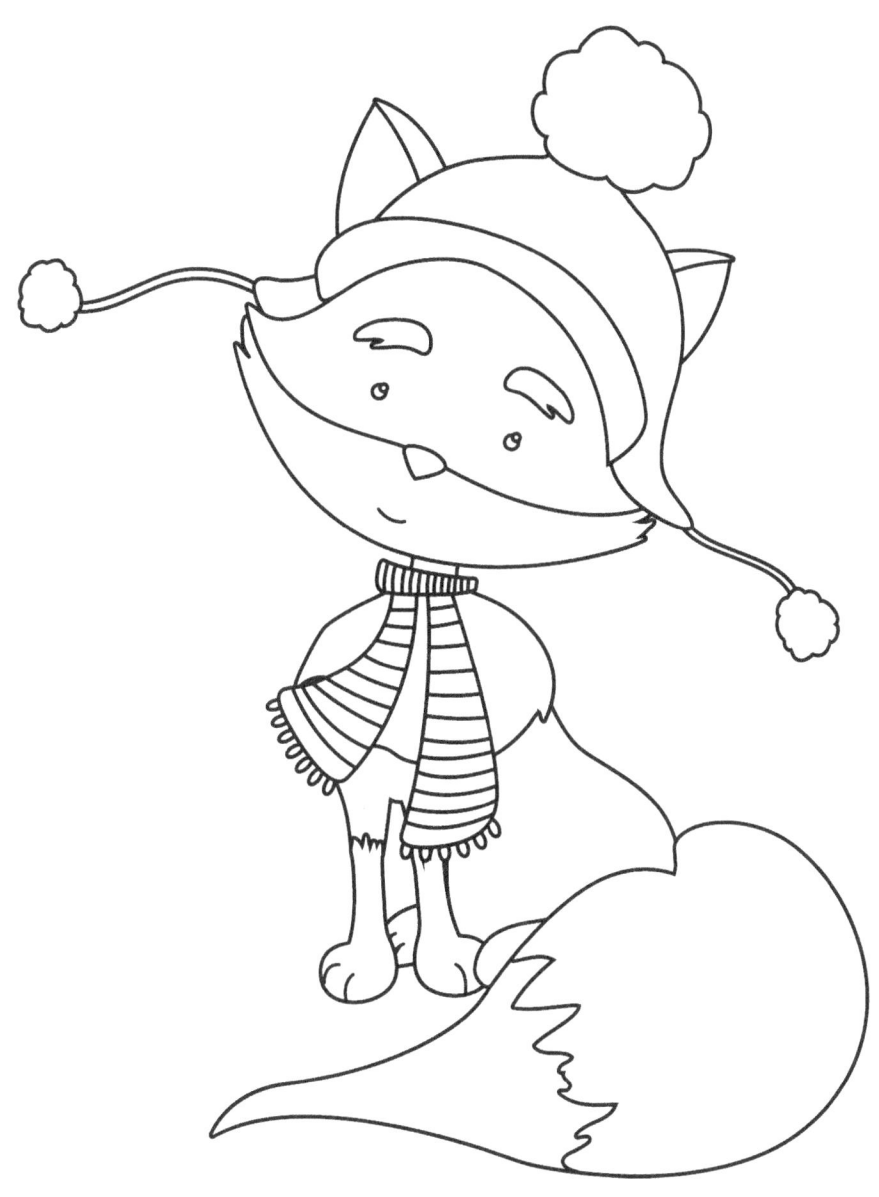

WOODLAND

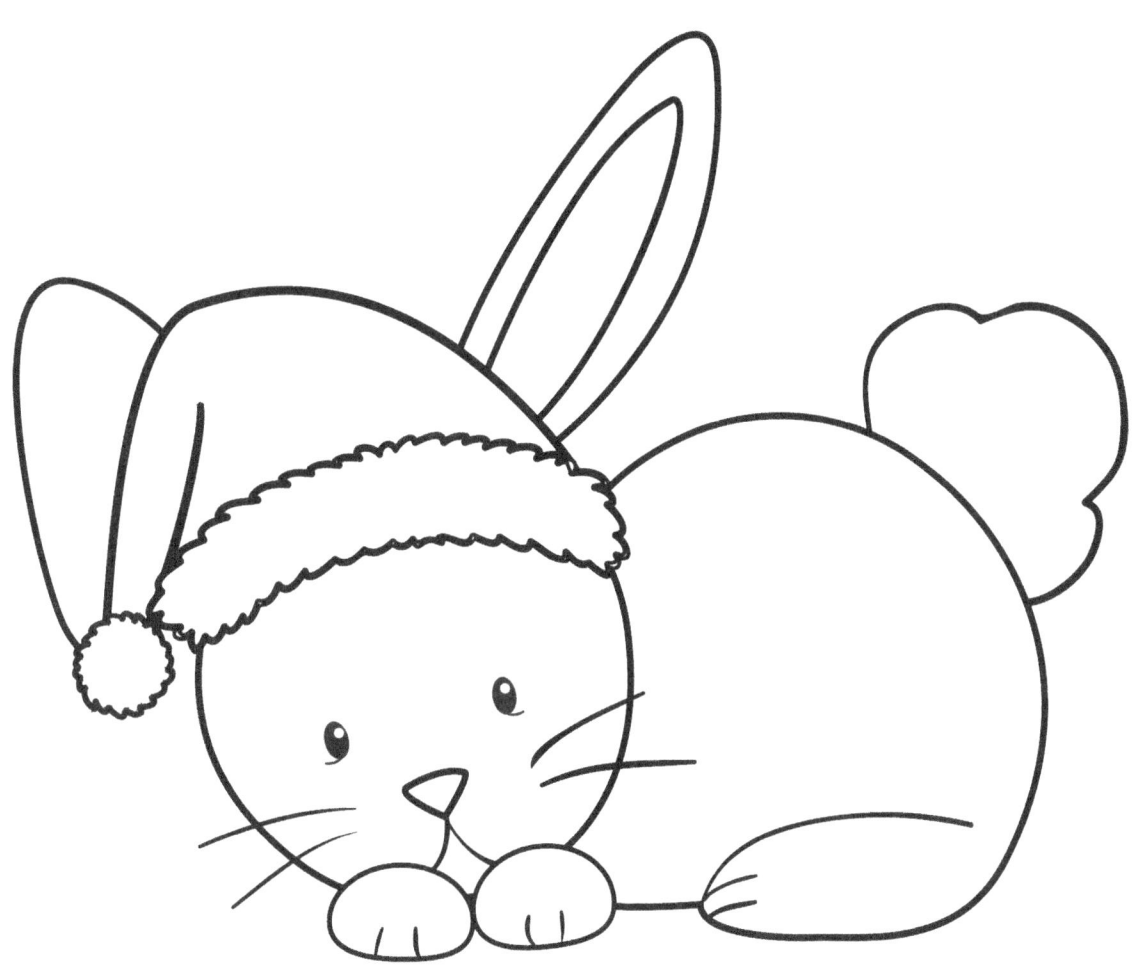

WOODLAND

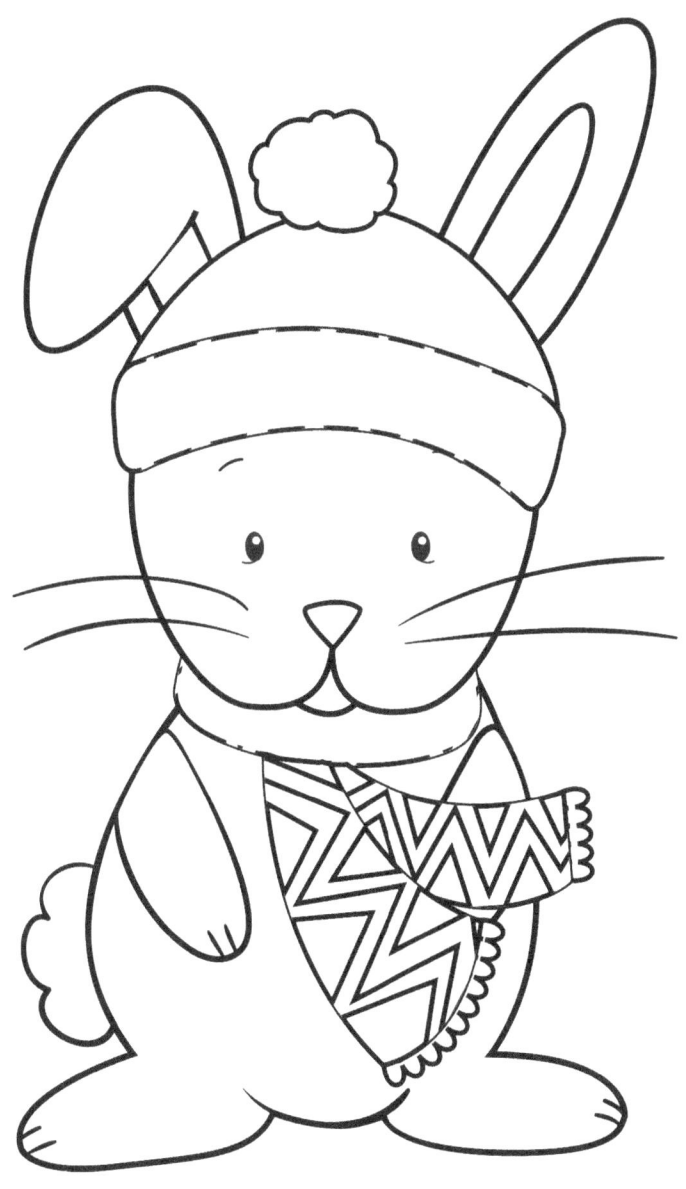

WOODLAND

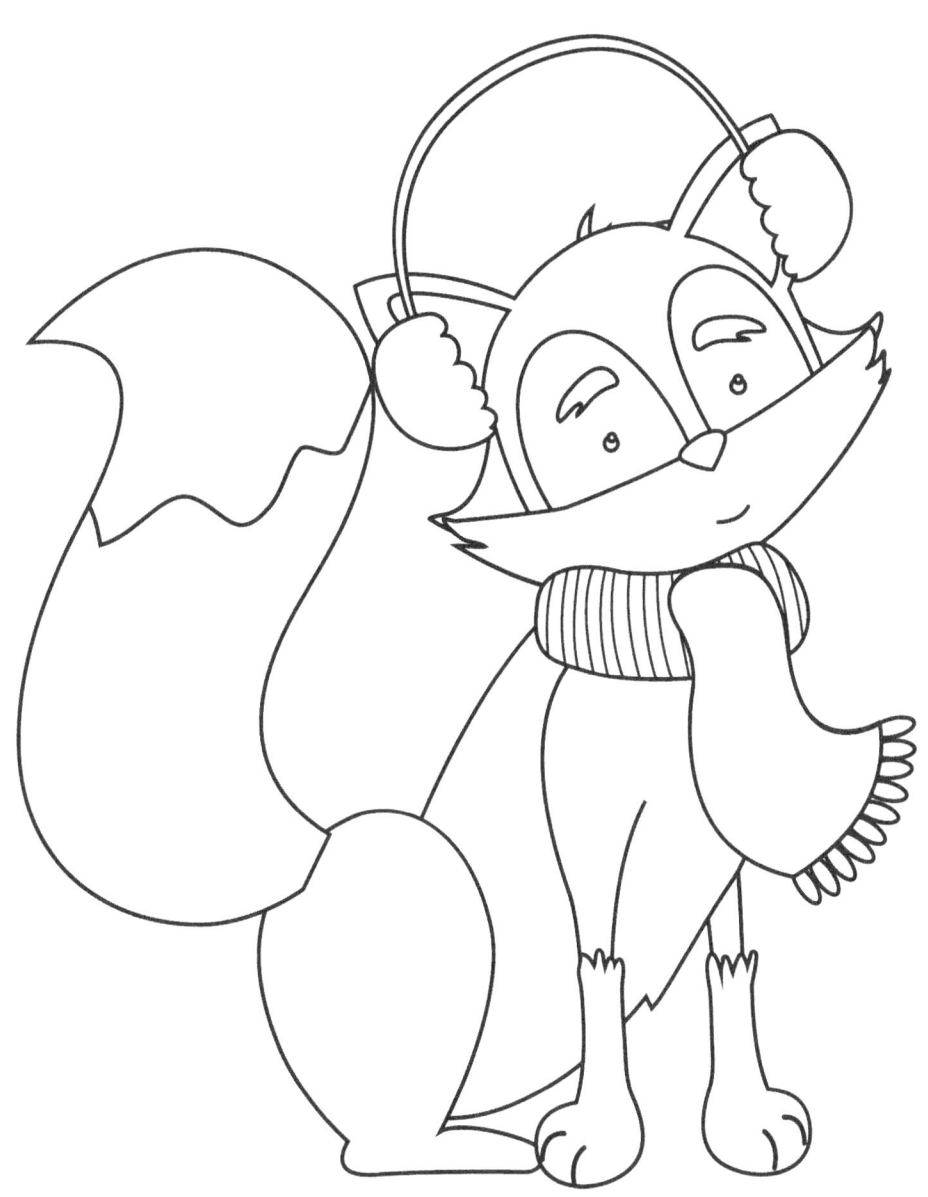

FAIRIES

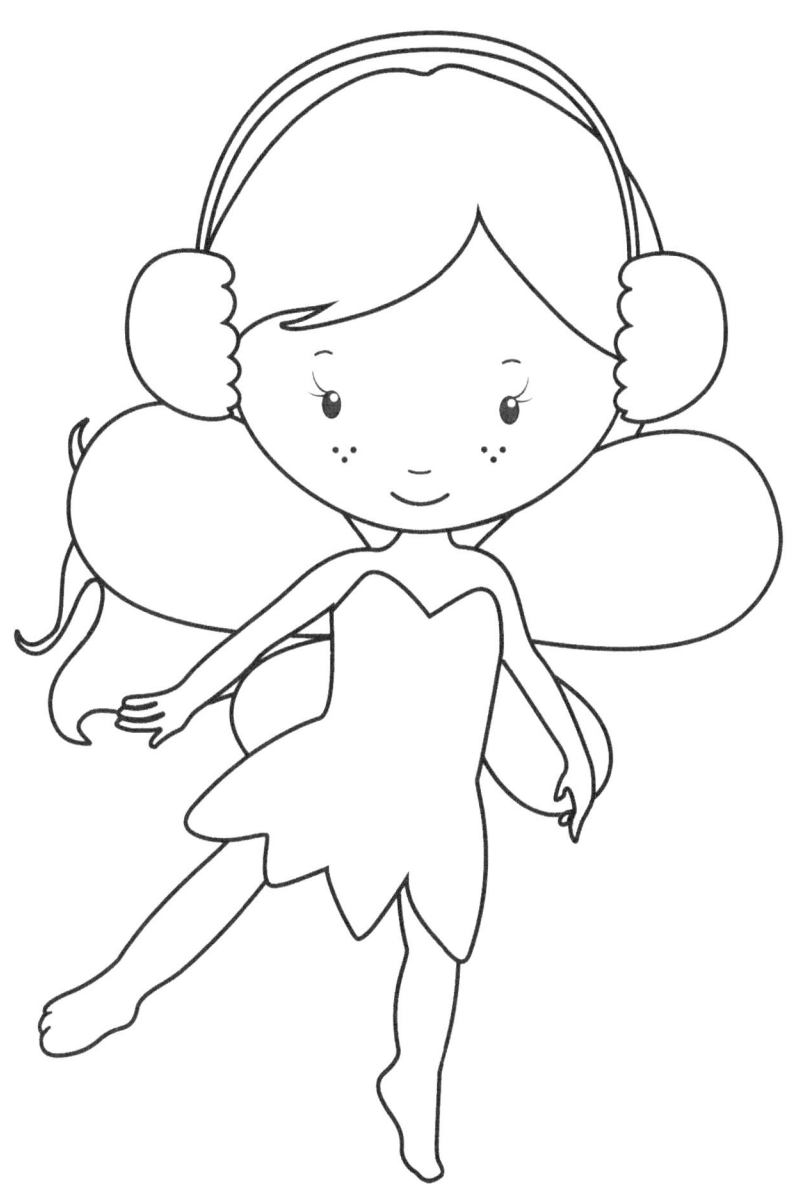

FAIRIES

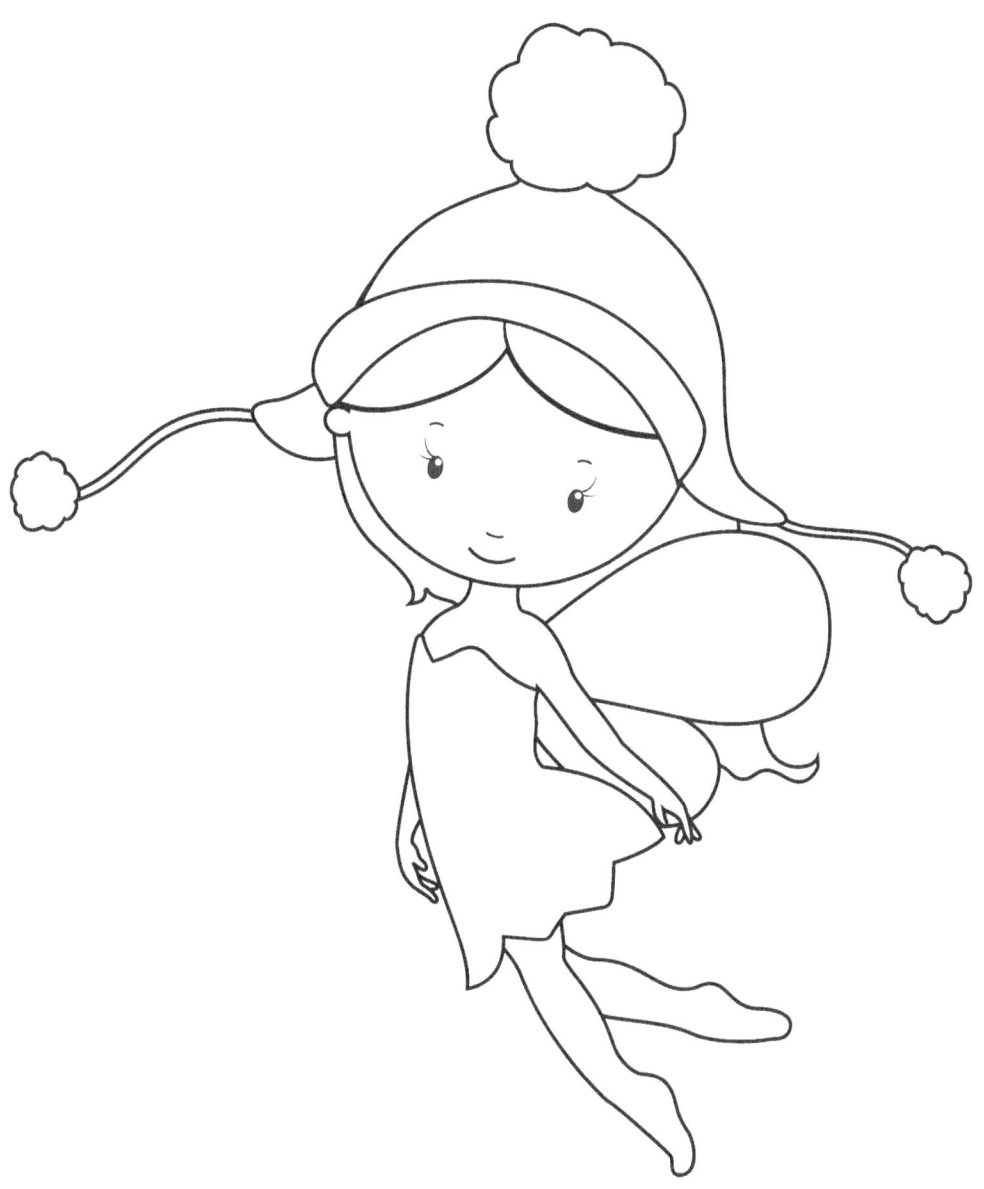

FAIRIES

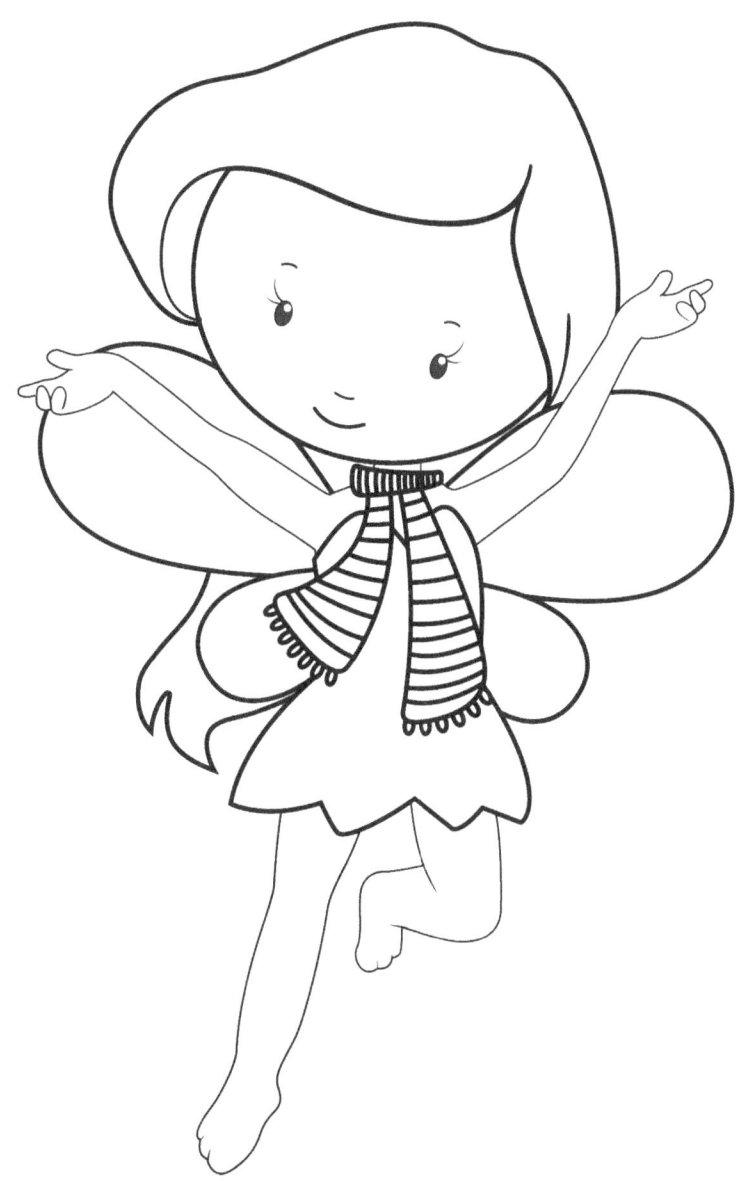

FAIRIES

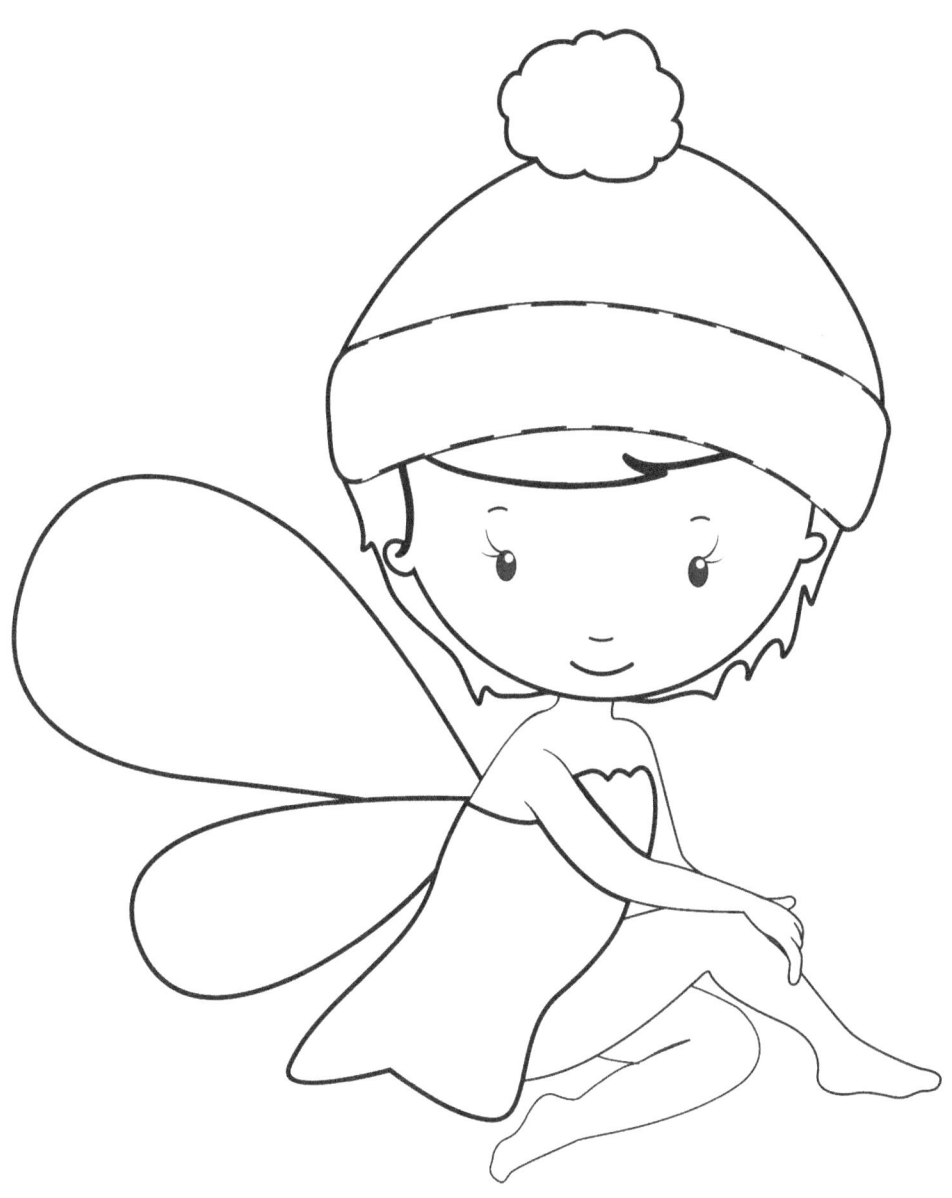

SANTA

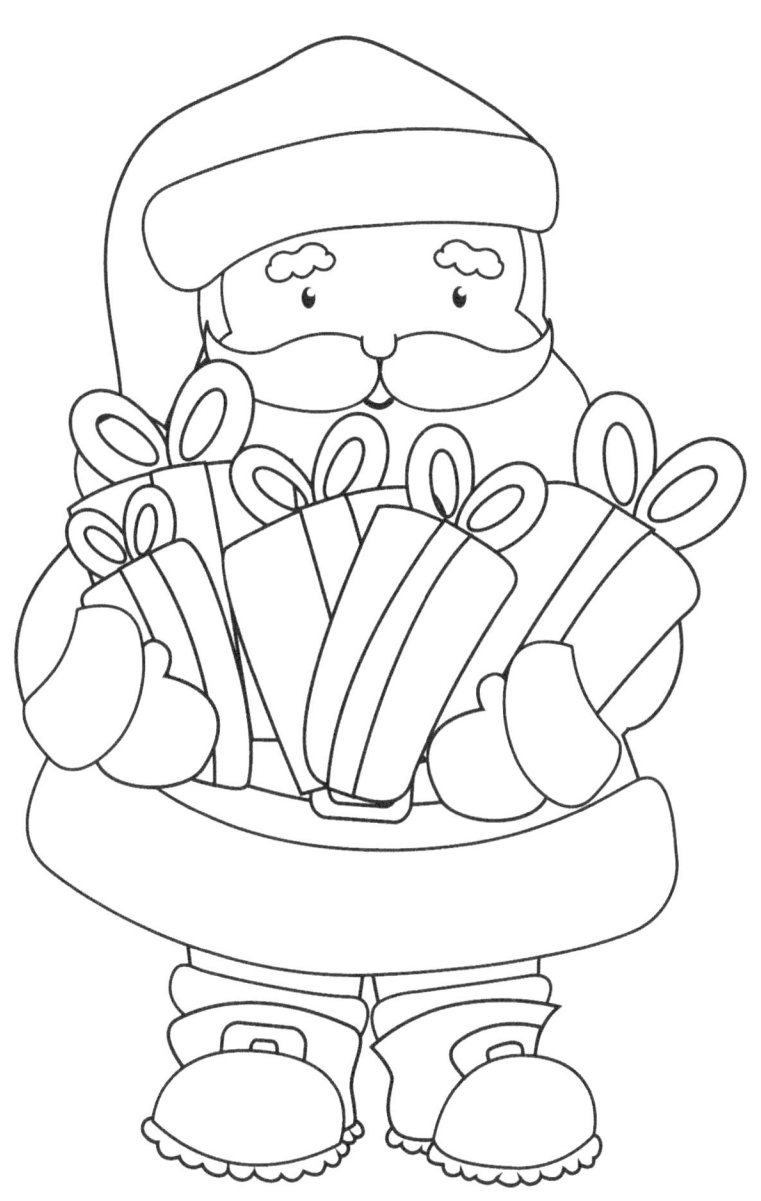

SANTA

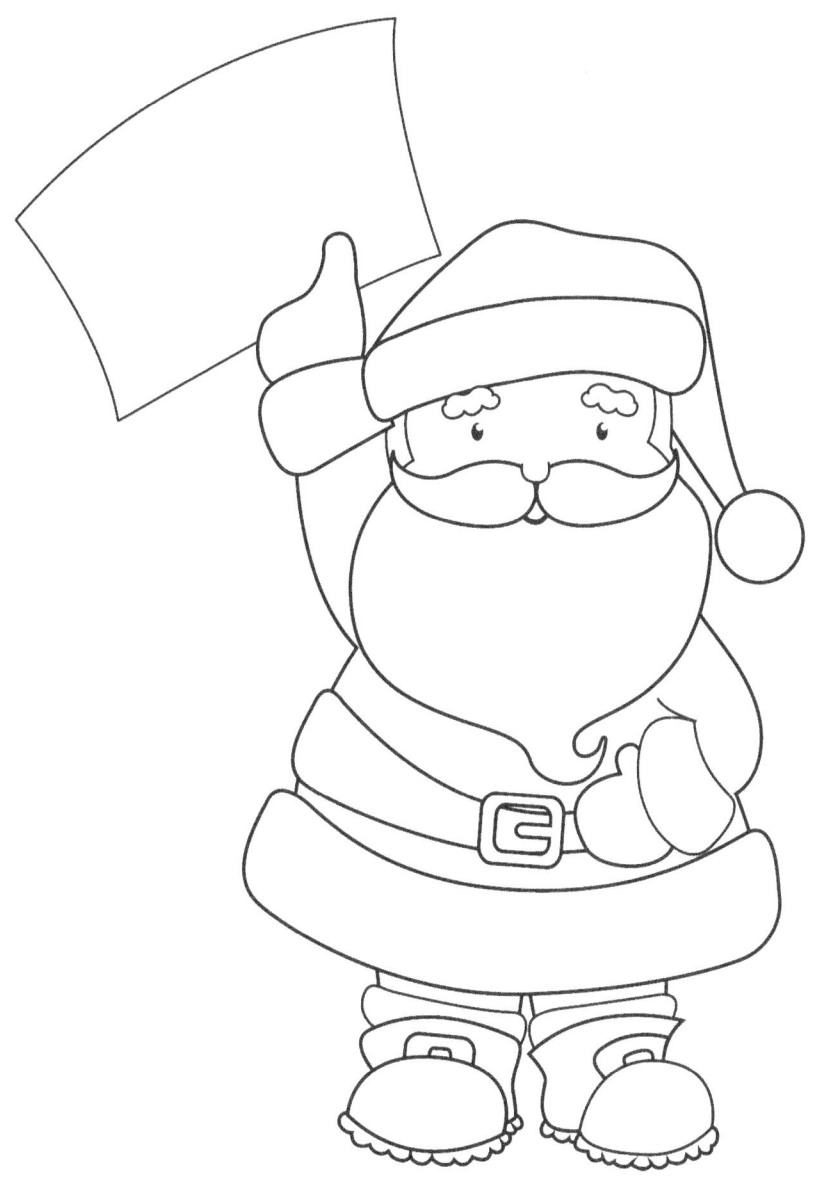

SANTA

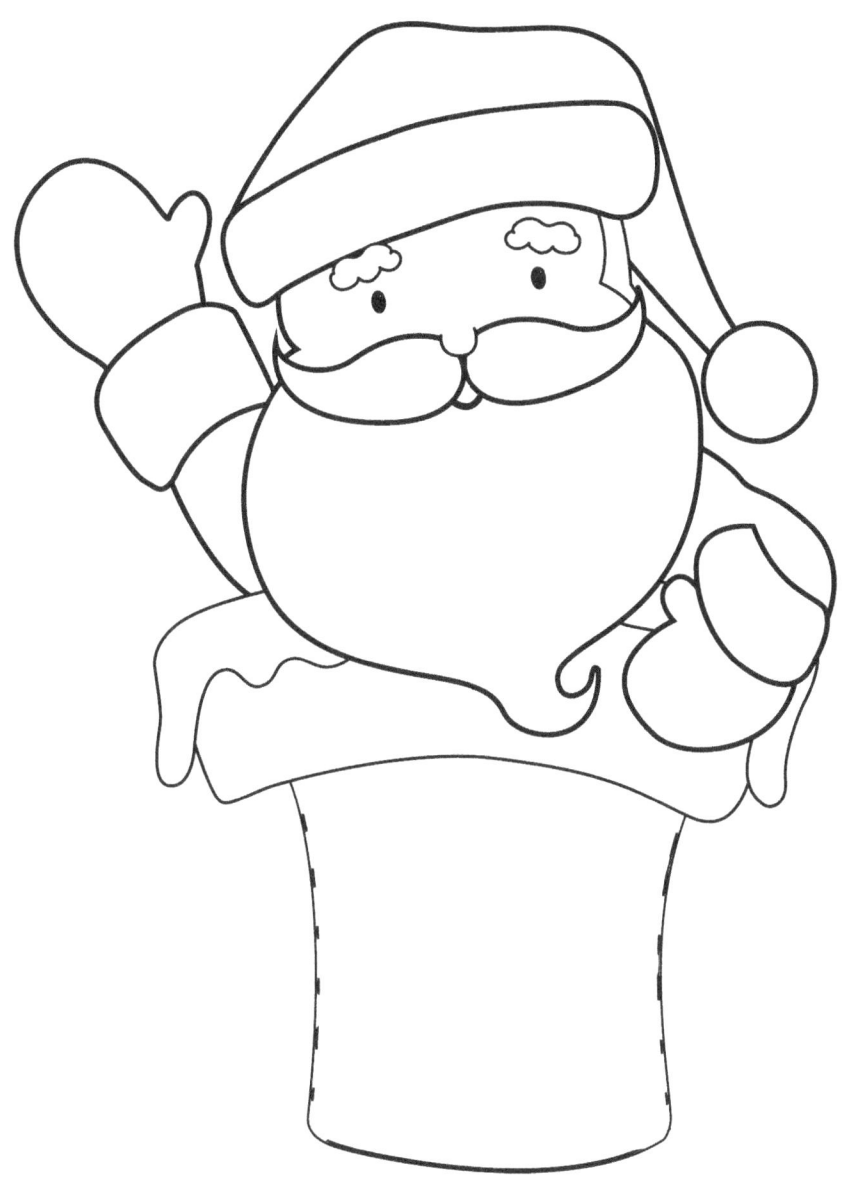

SANTA

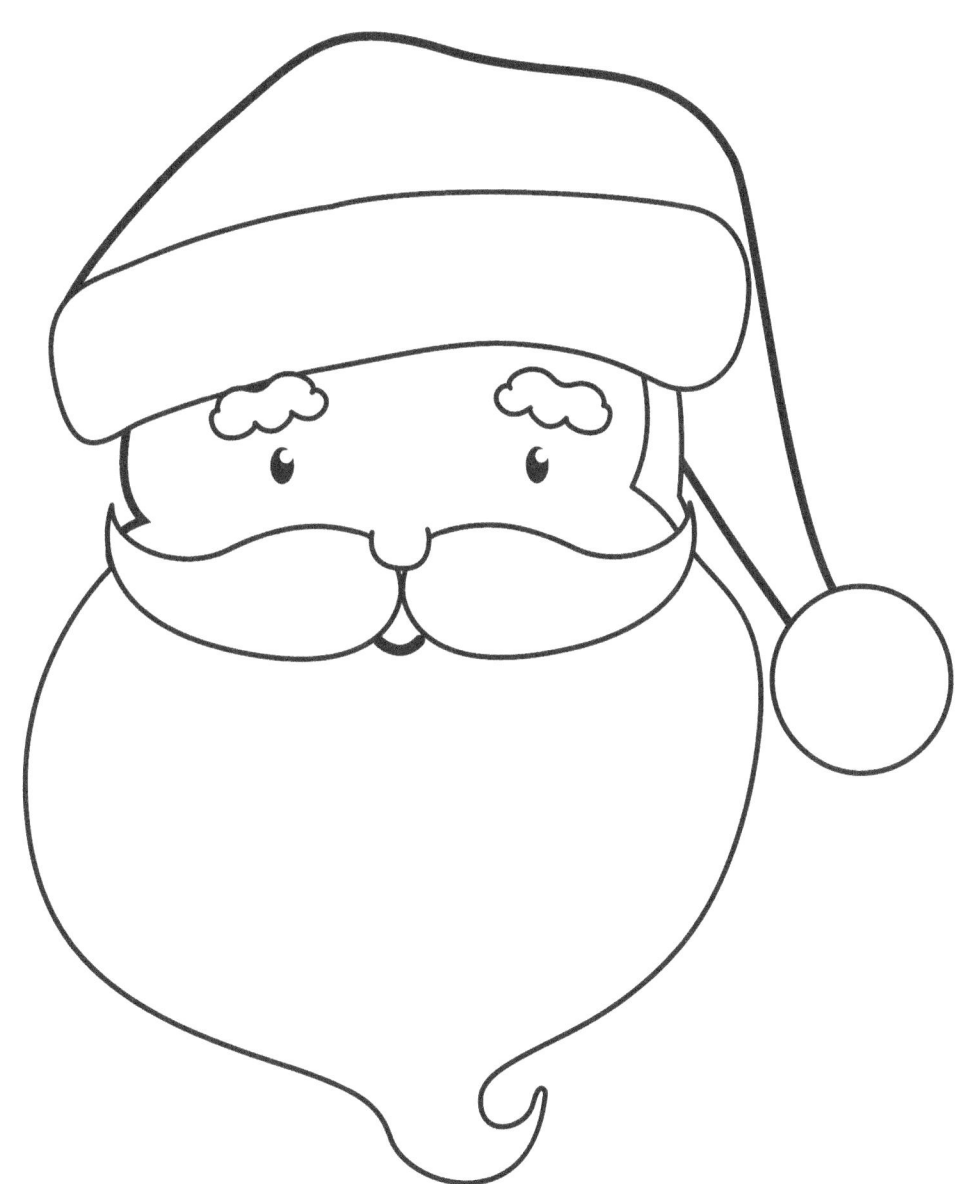

SANTA

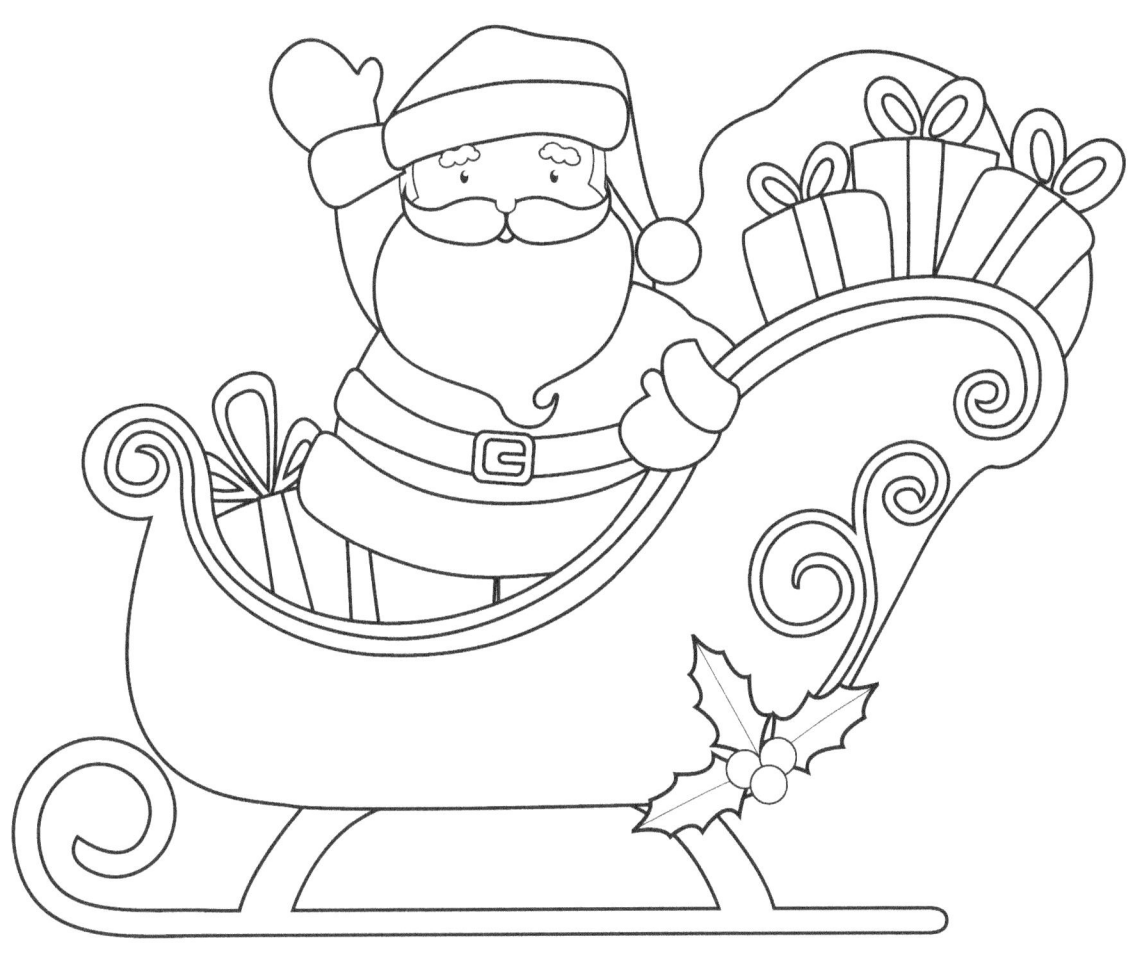

BEAR

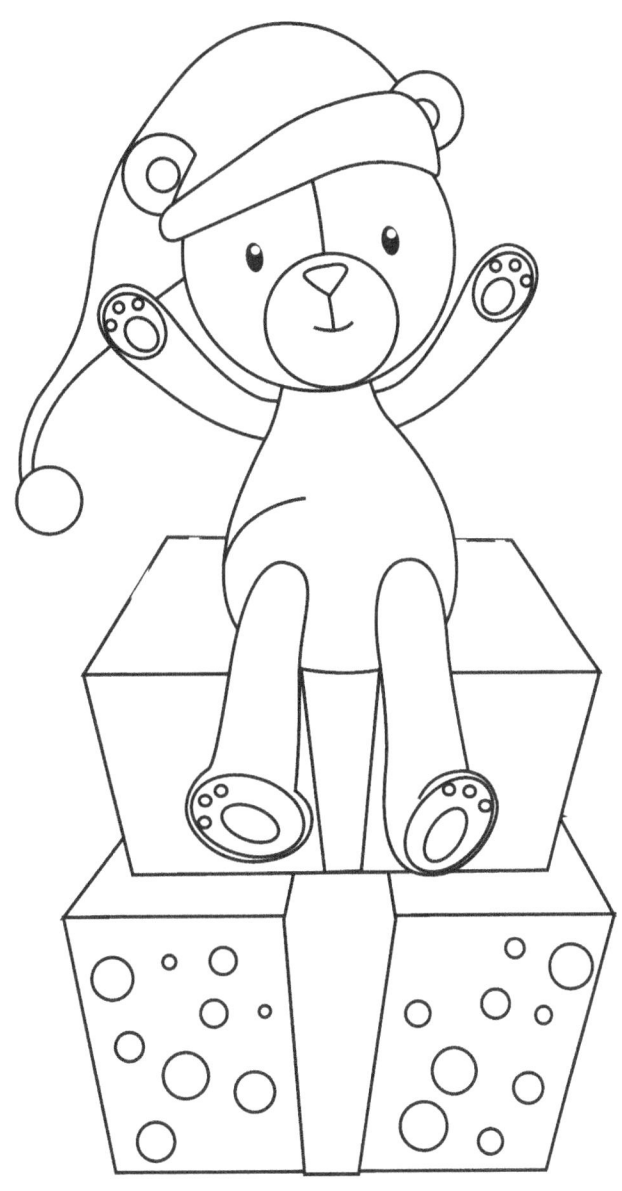

BEAR

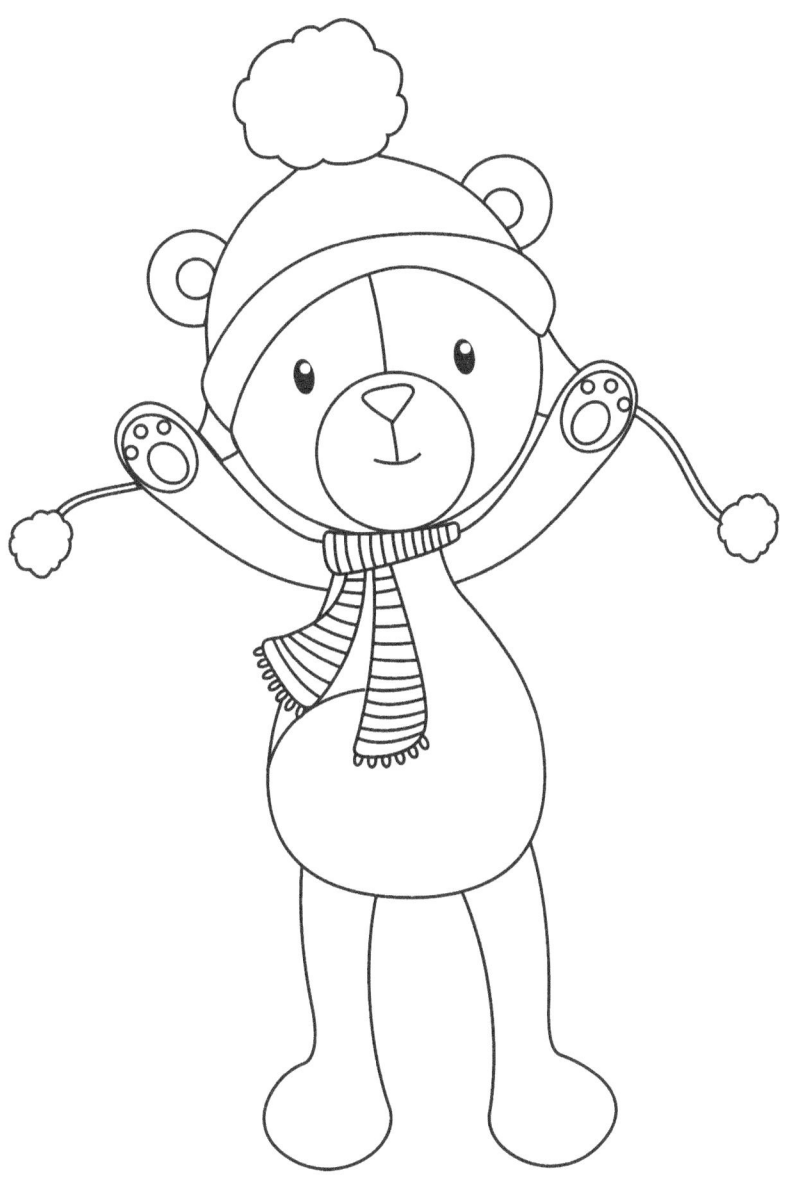

BEAR

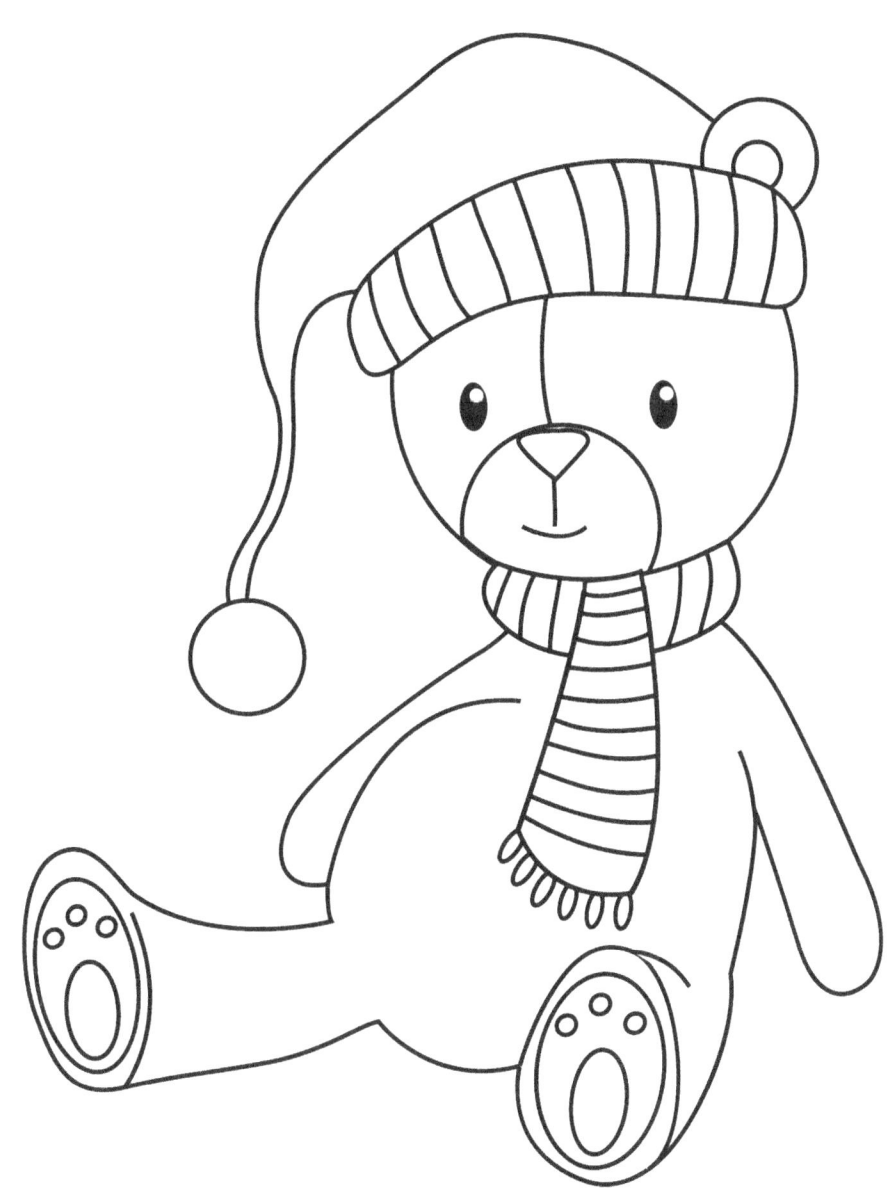

BEAR

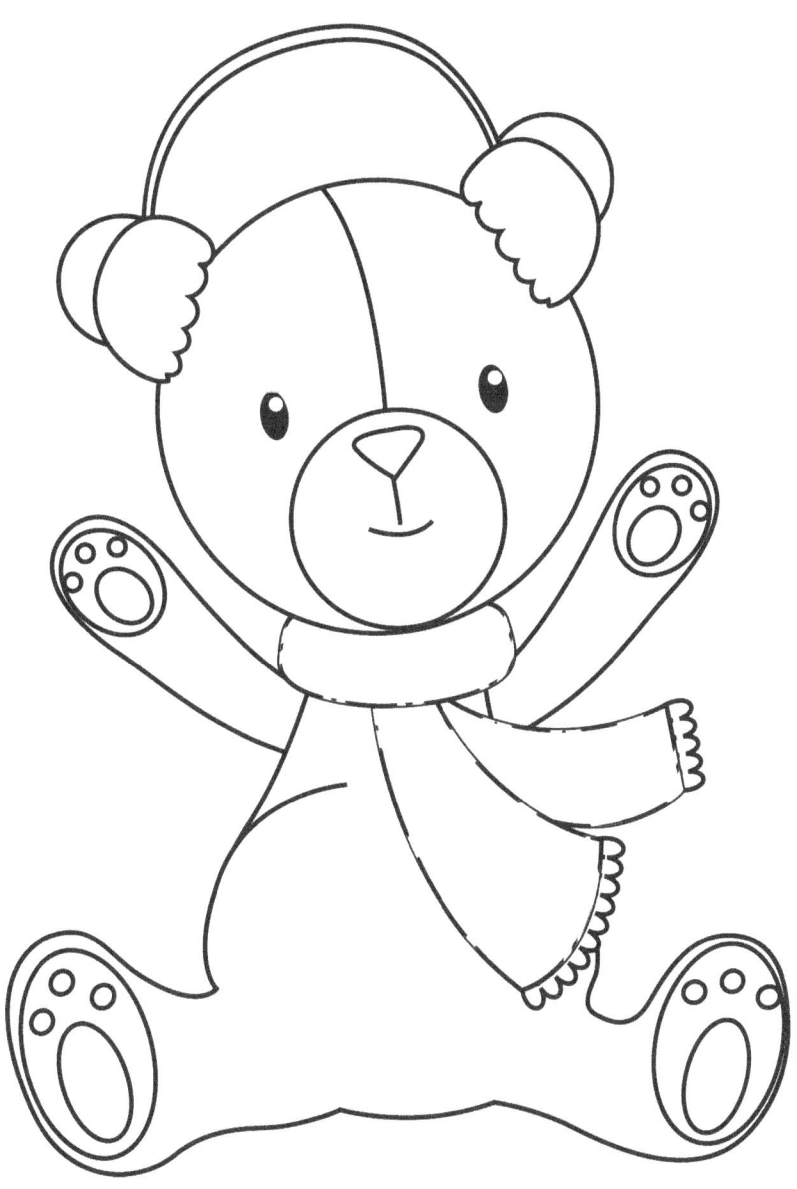

BEAR

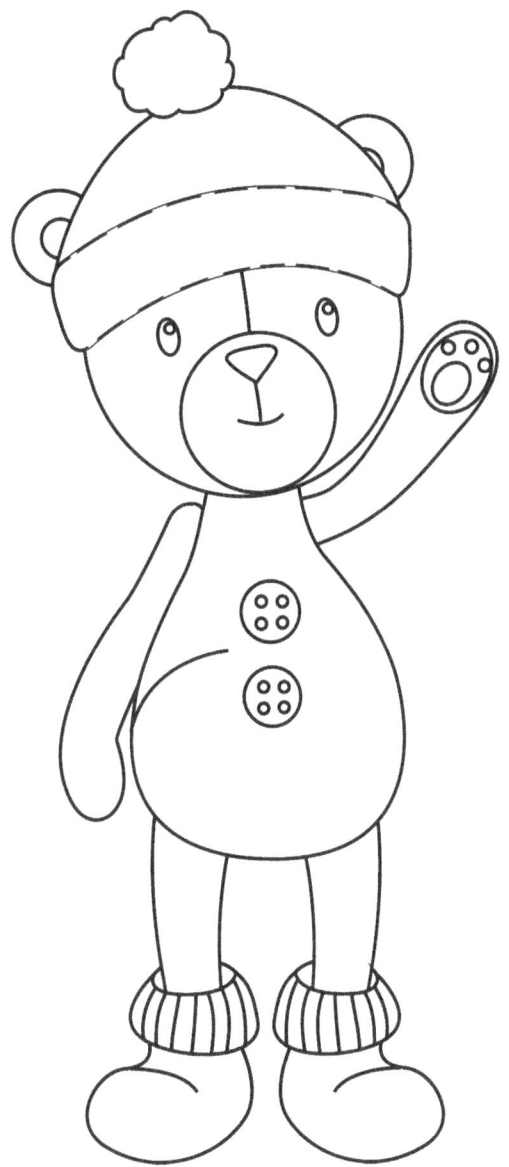

BEAR

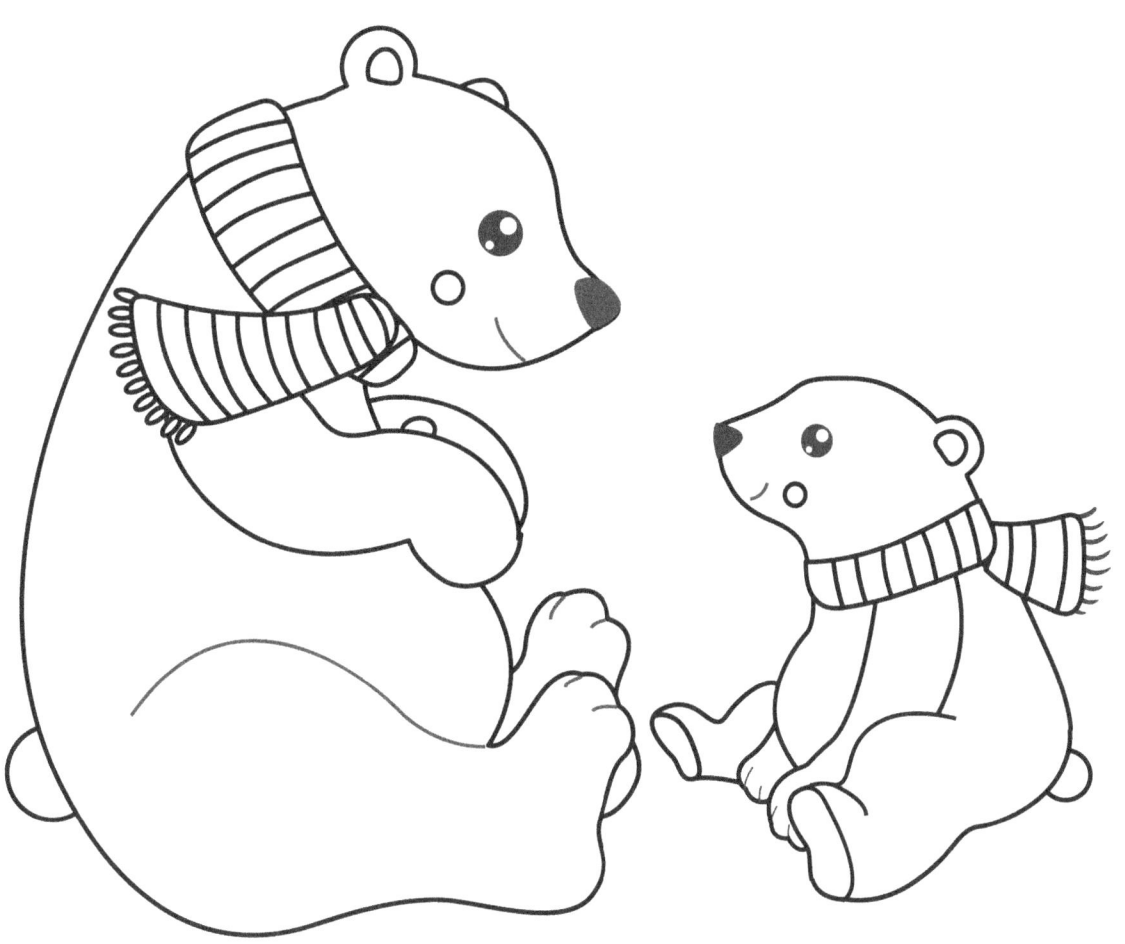

BEAR

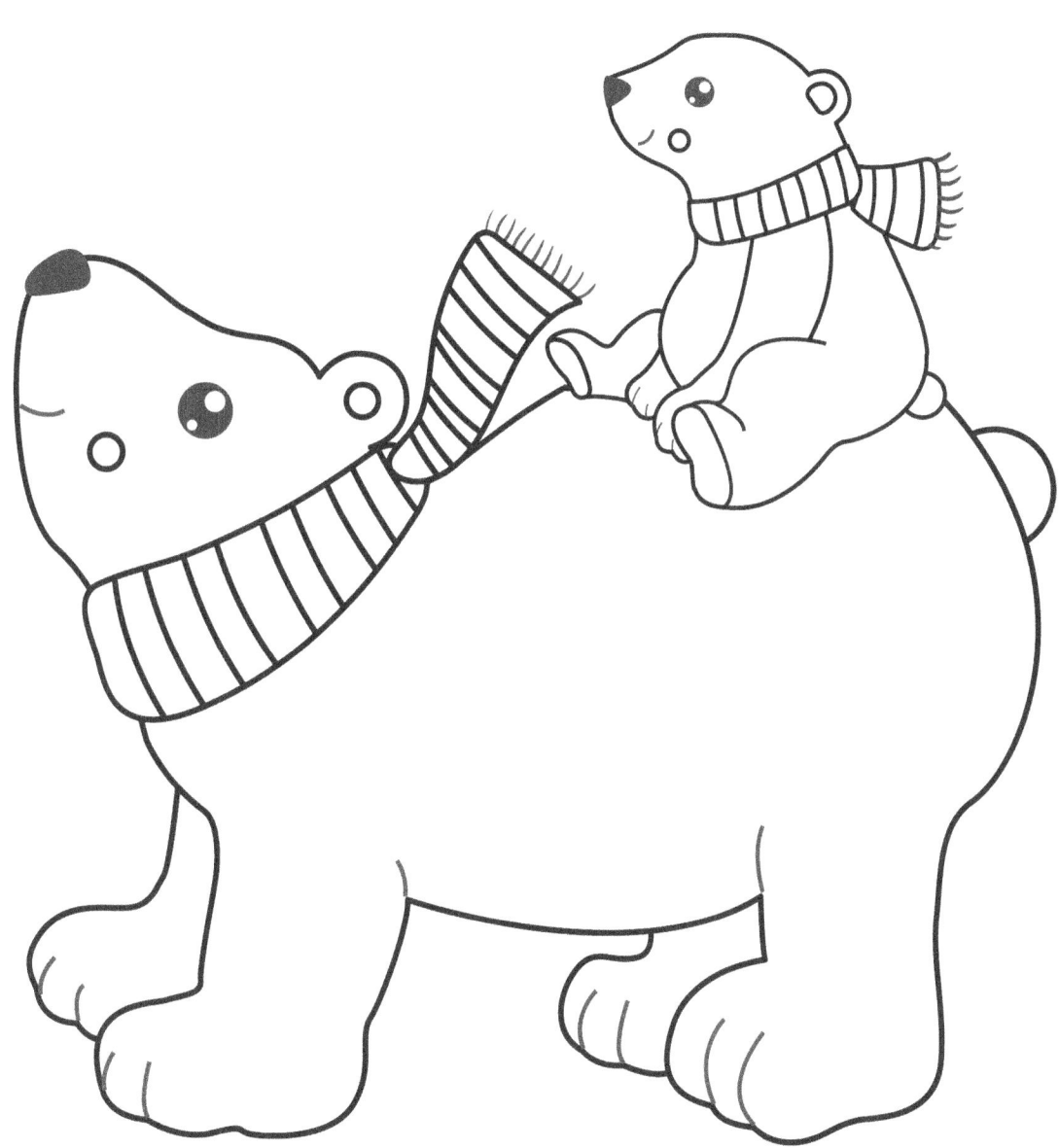

BEAR

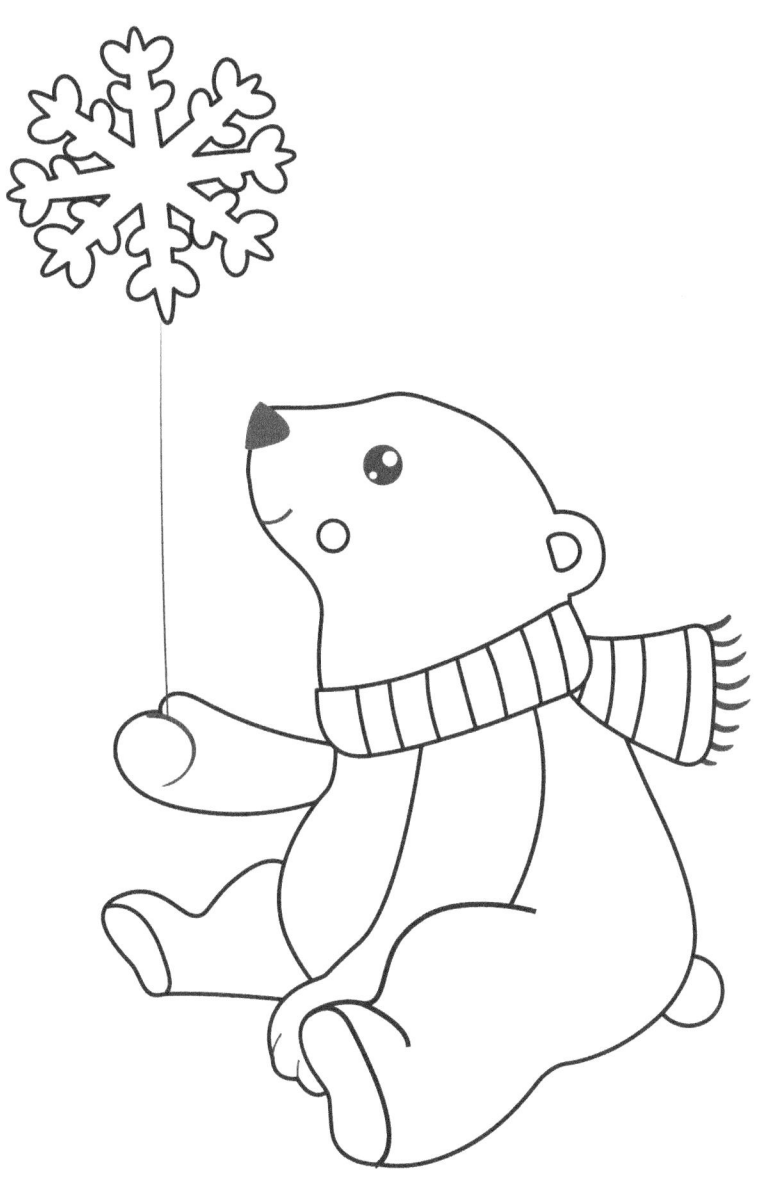

BEAR

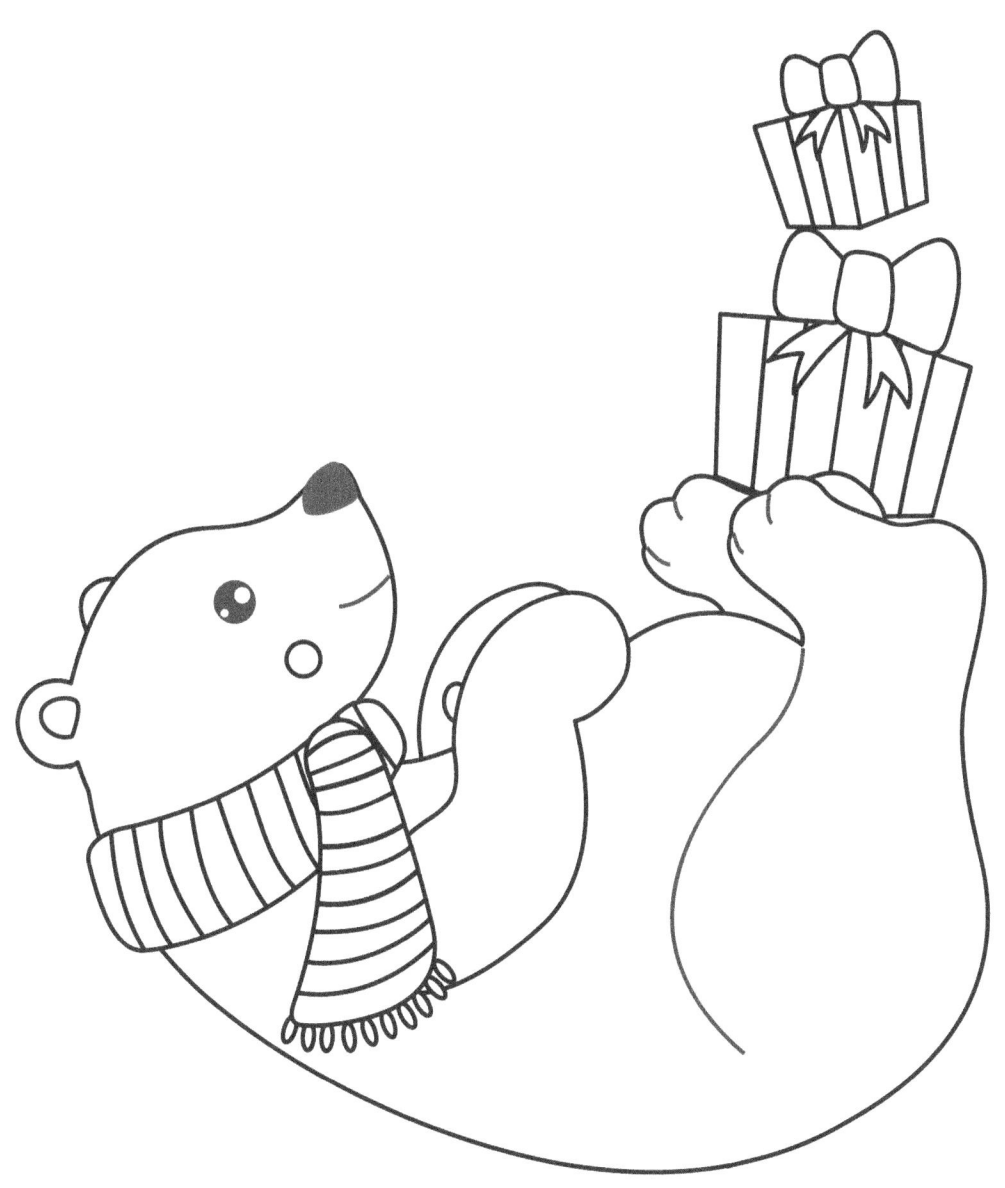

BEAR

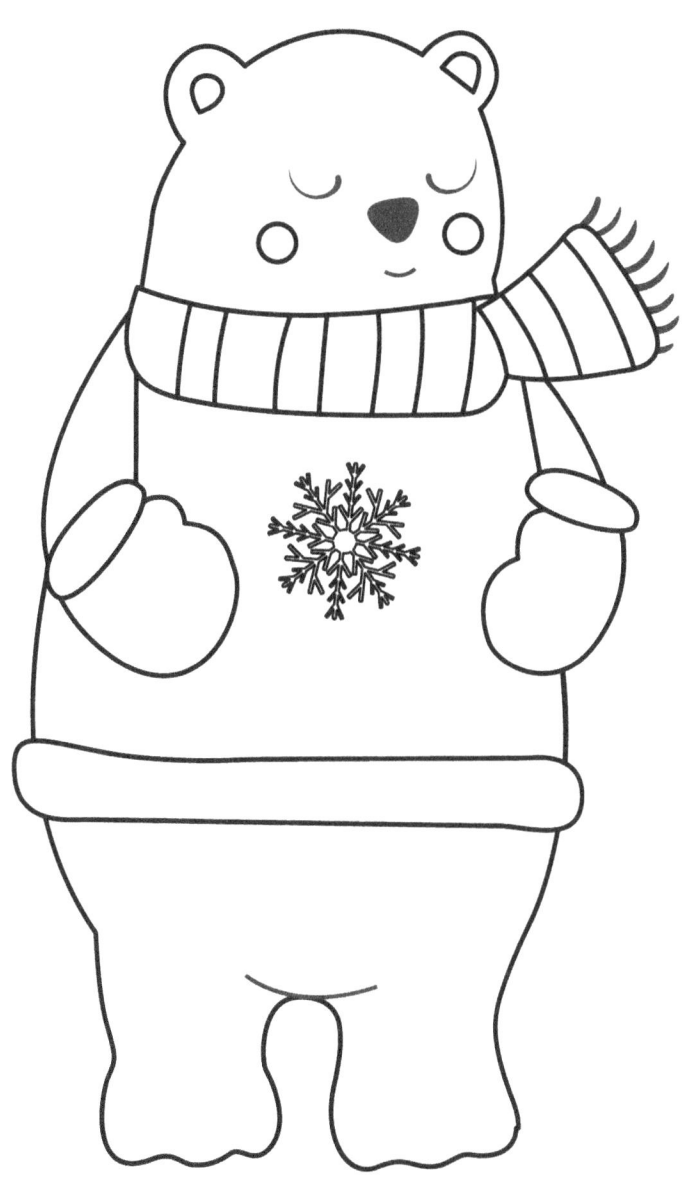

NUTCRACKER

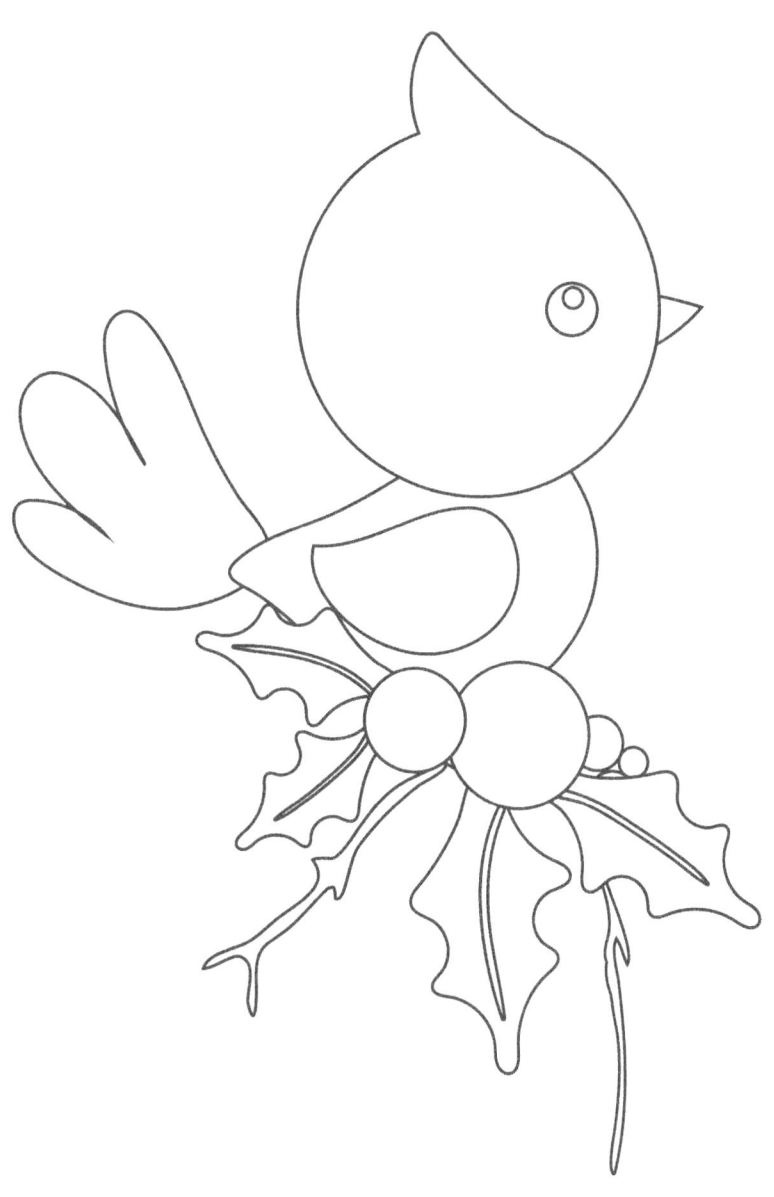

NUTCRACKER

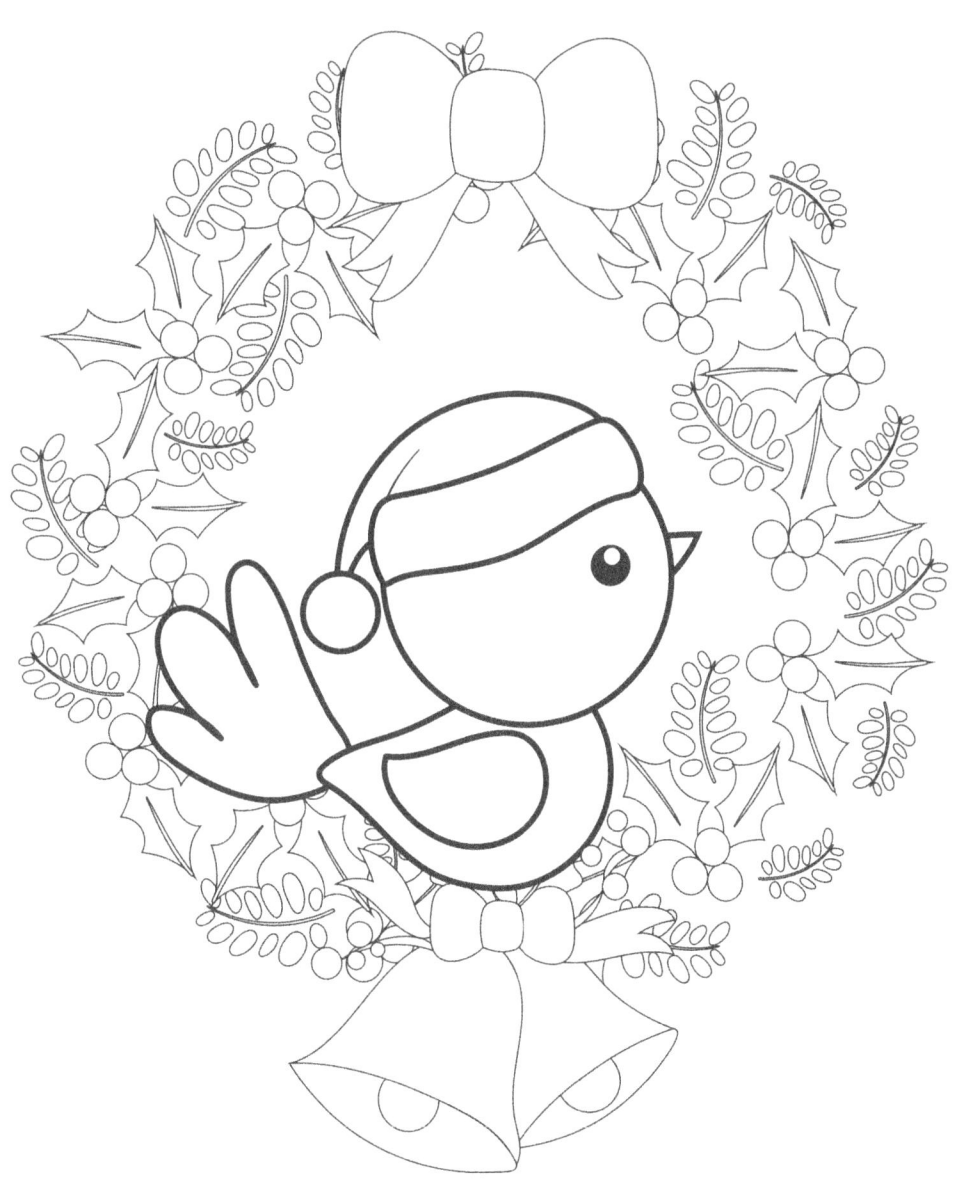

NUTCRACKER

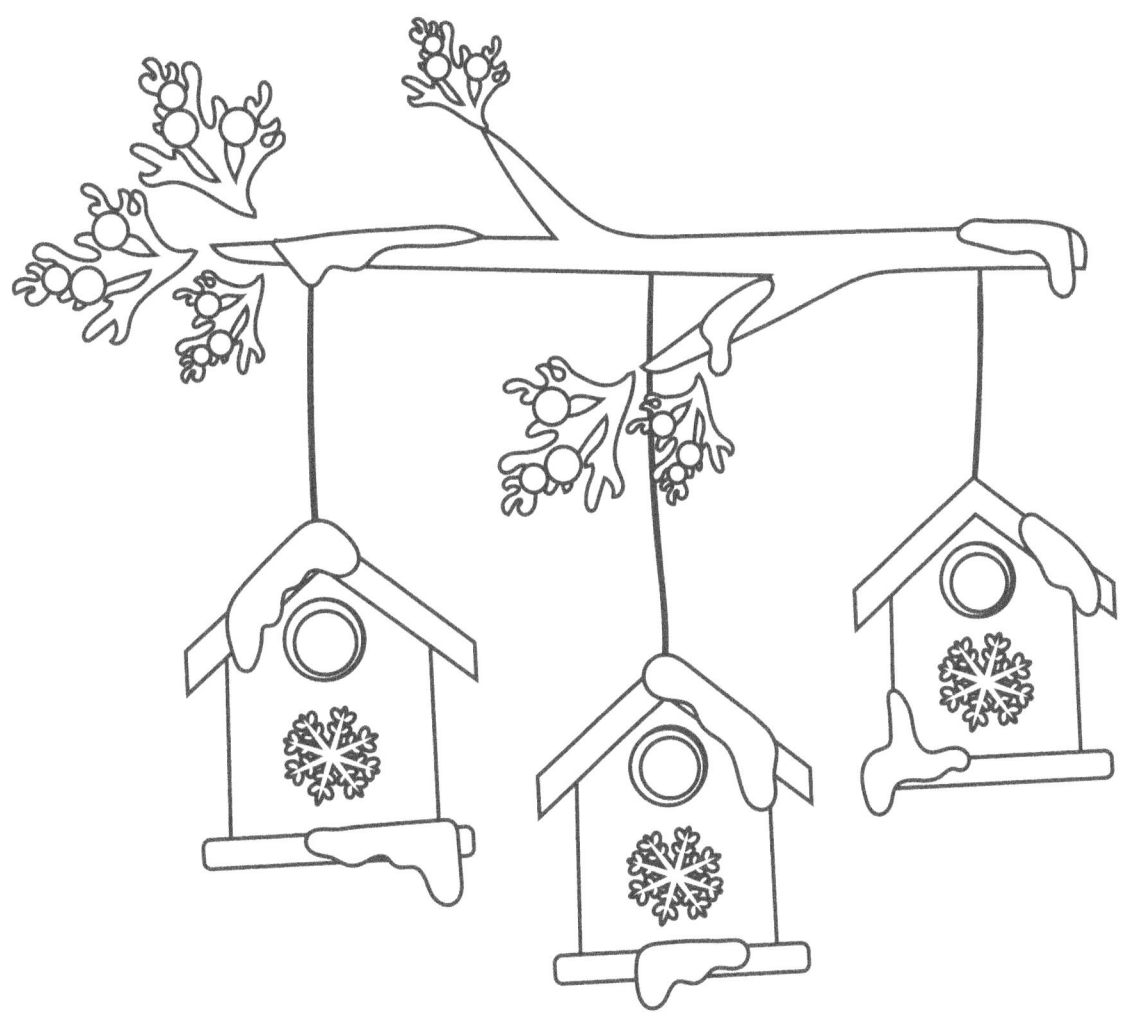

NUTCRACKER

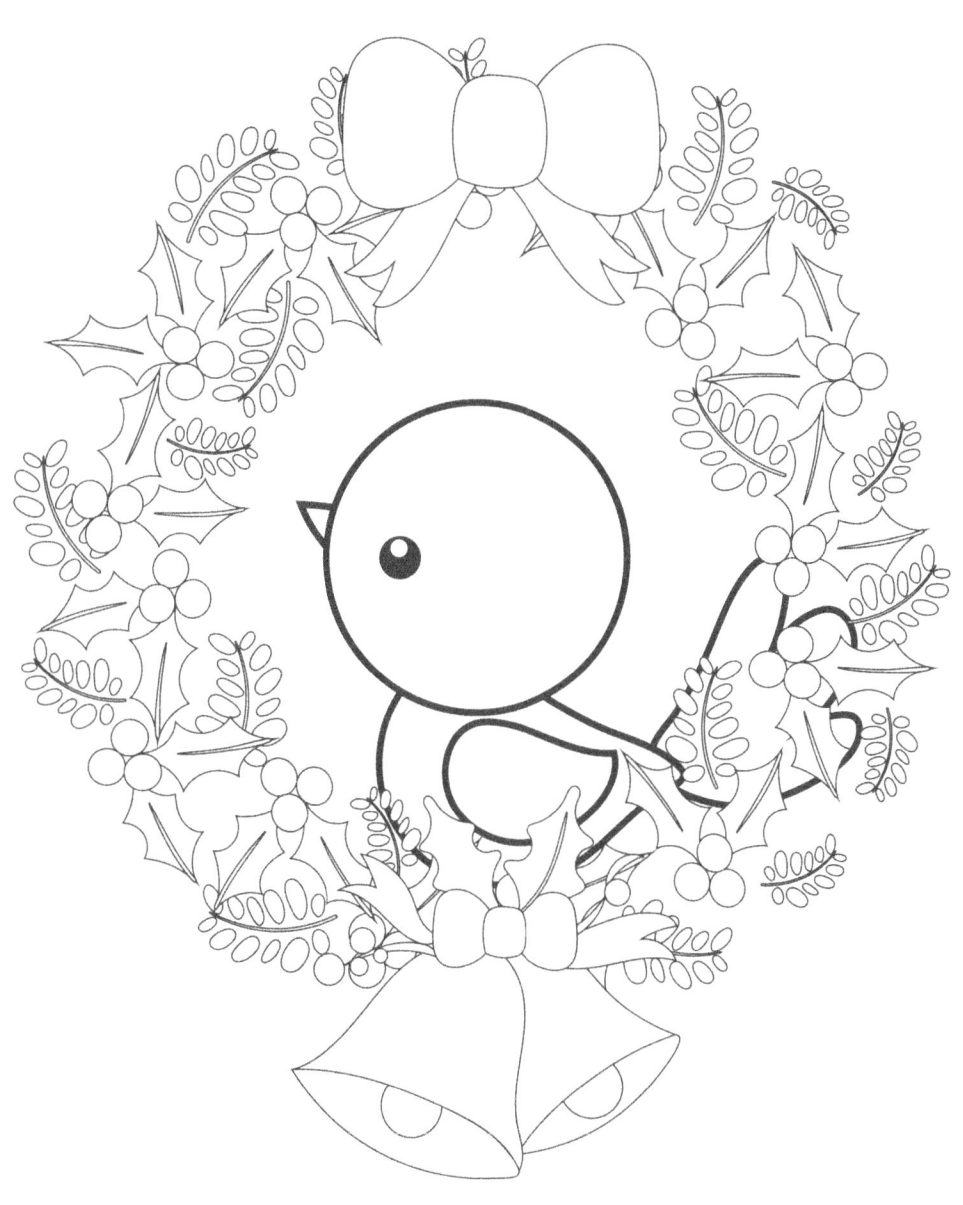

NUTCRACKER

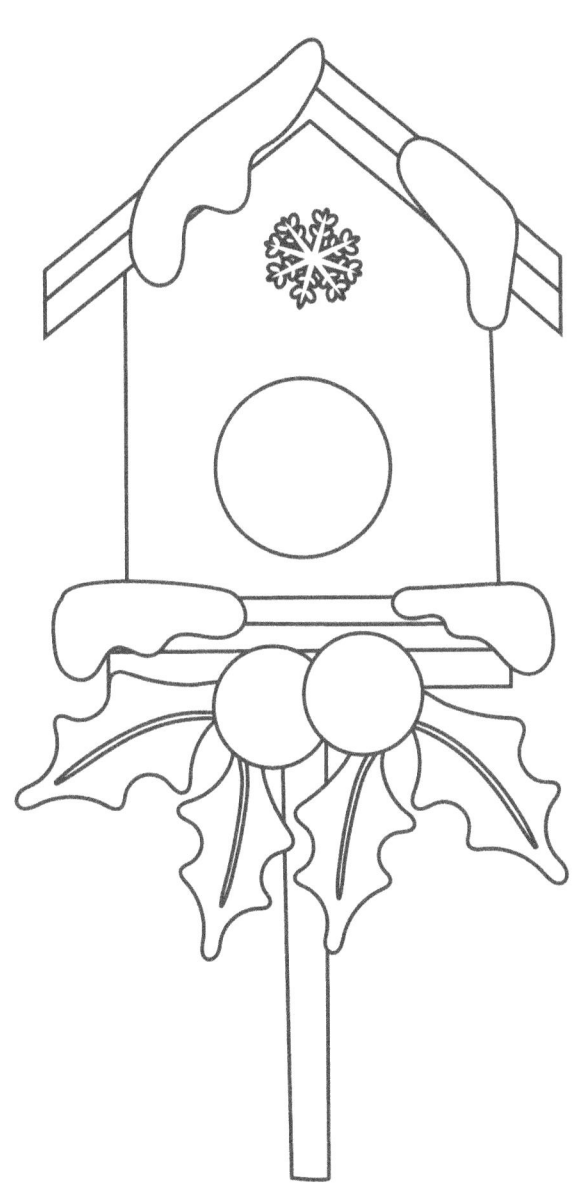

NUTCRACKER

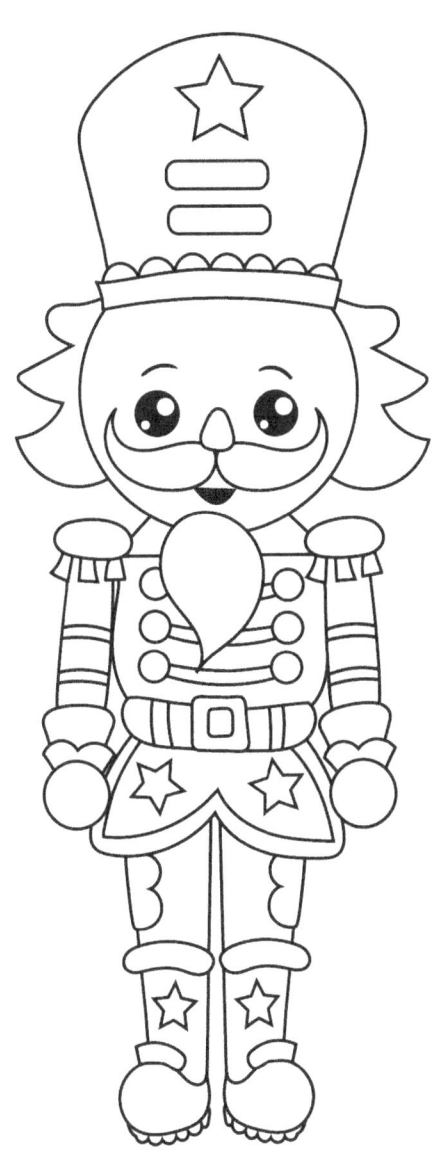

NUTCRACKER

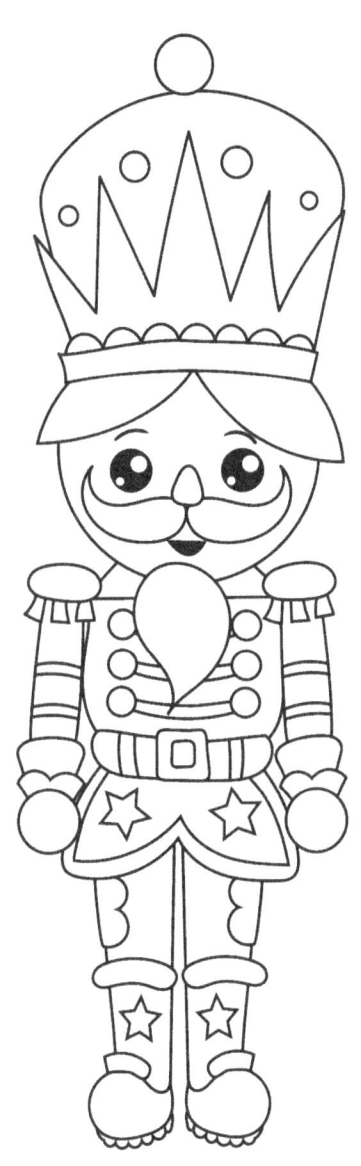

NUTCRACKER

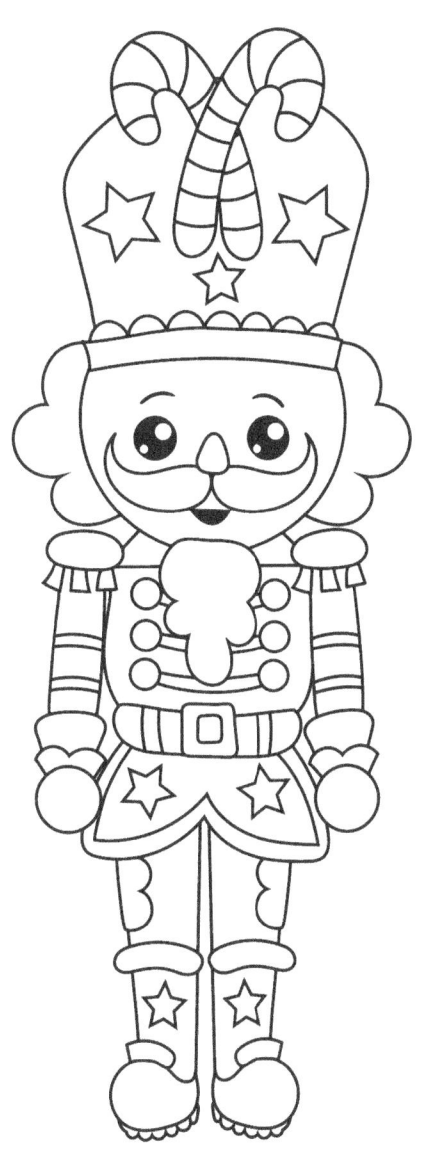

NUTCRACKER

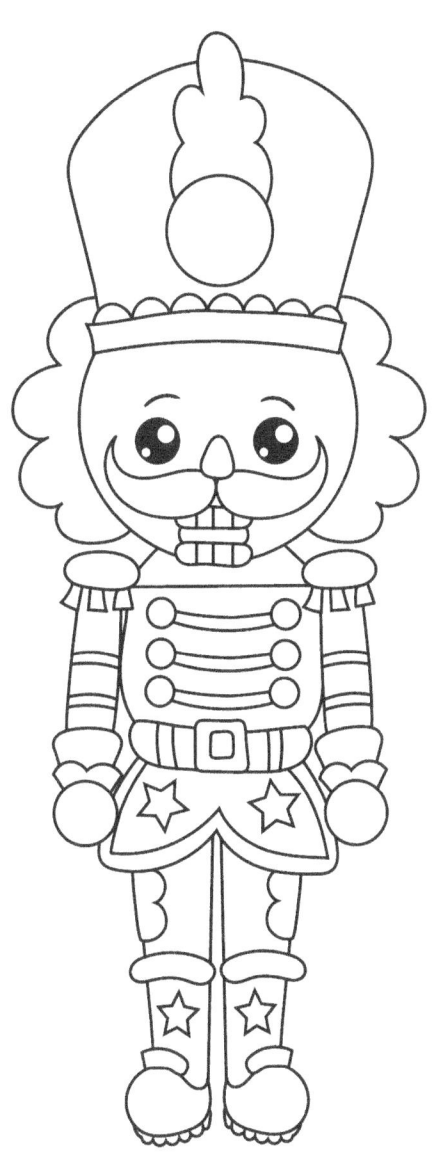

SANTA VACATION

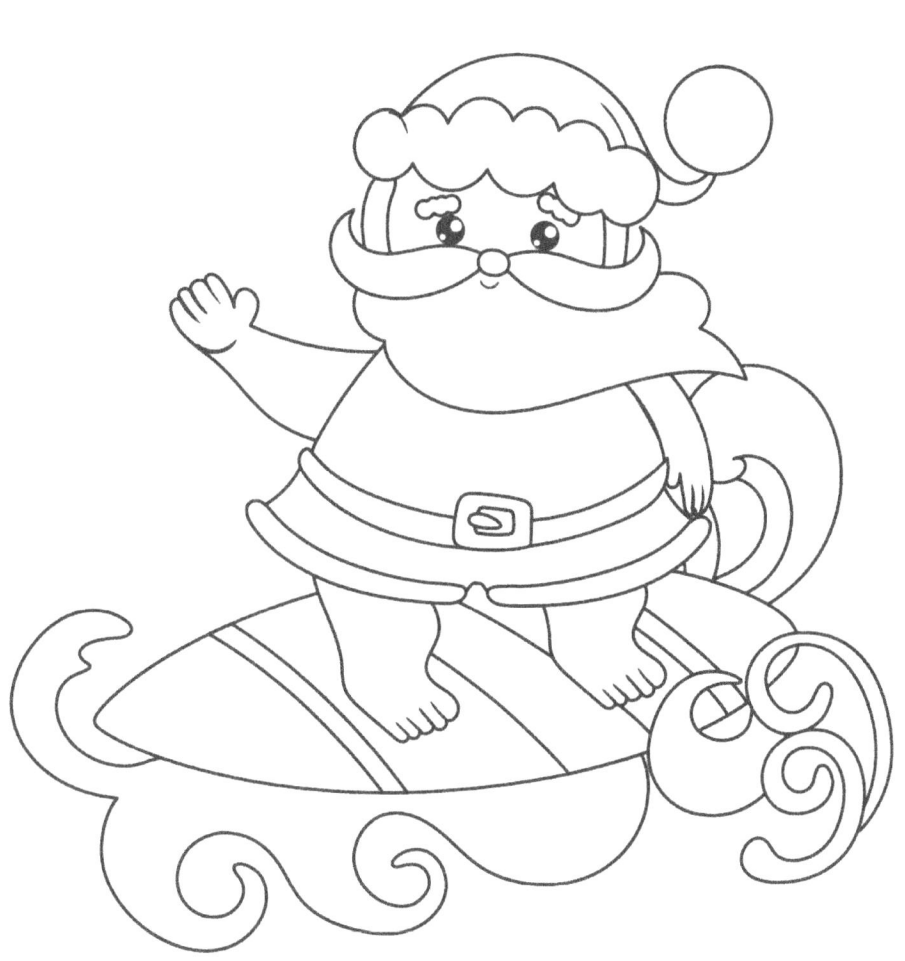

SANTA VACATION

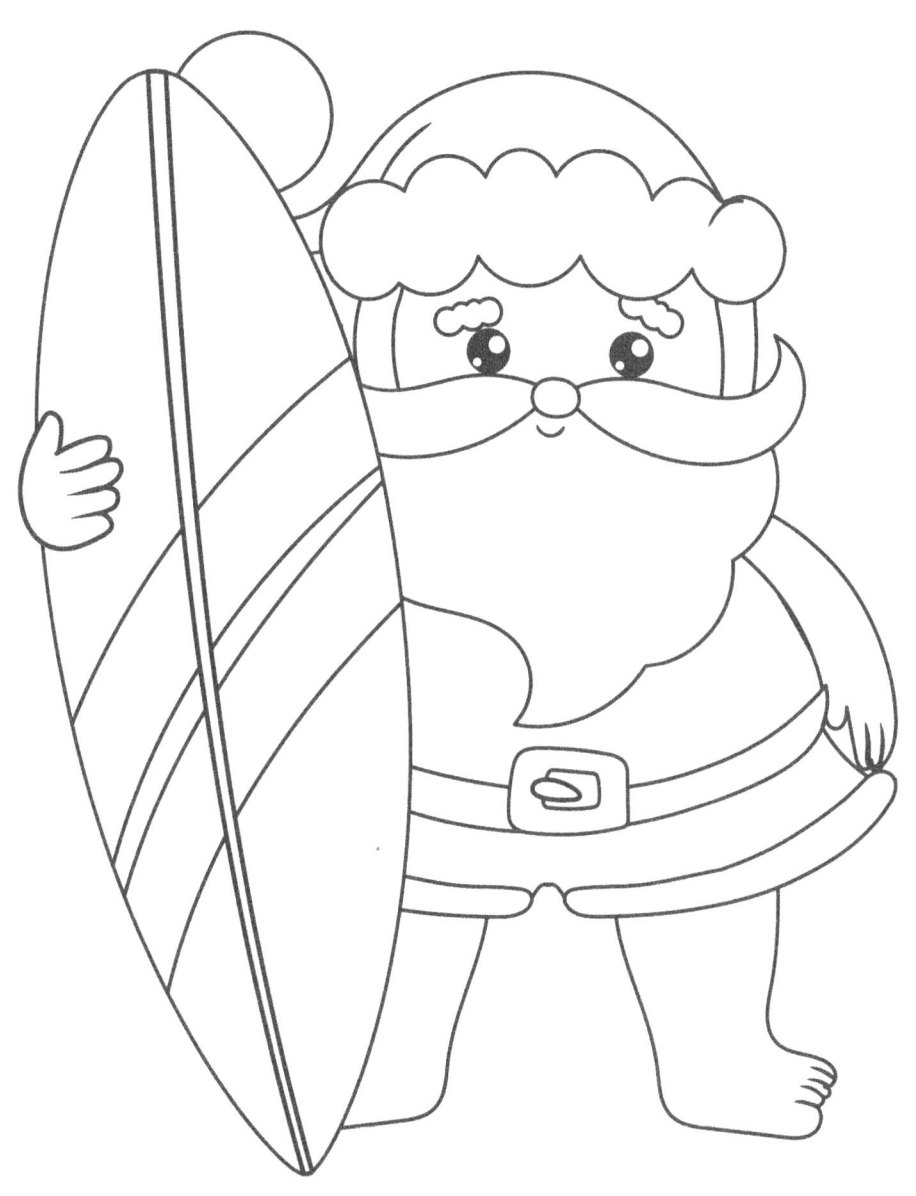

SANTA VACATION

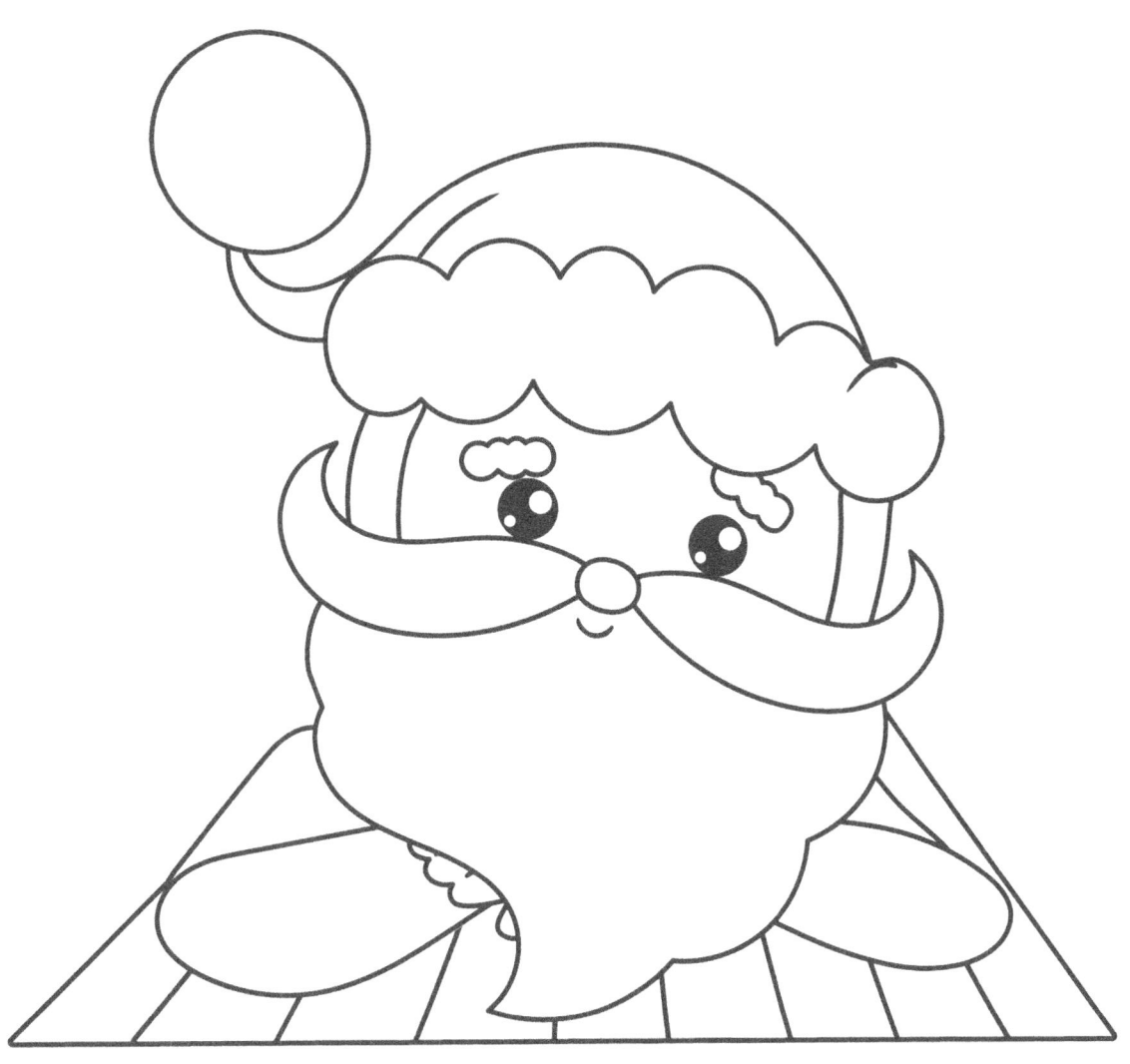

SANTA VACATION

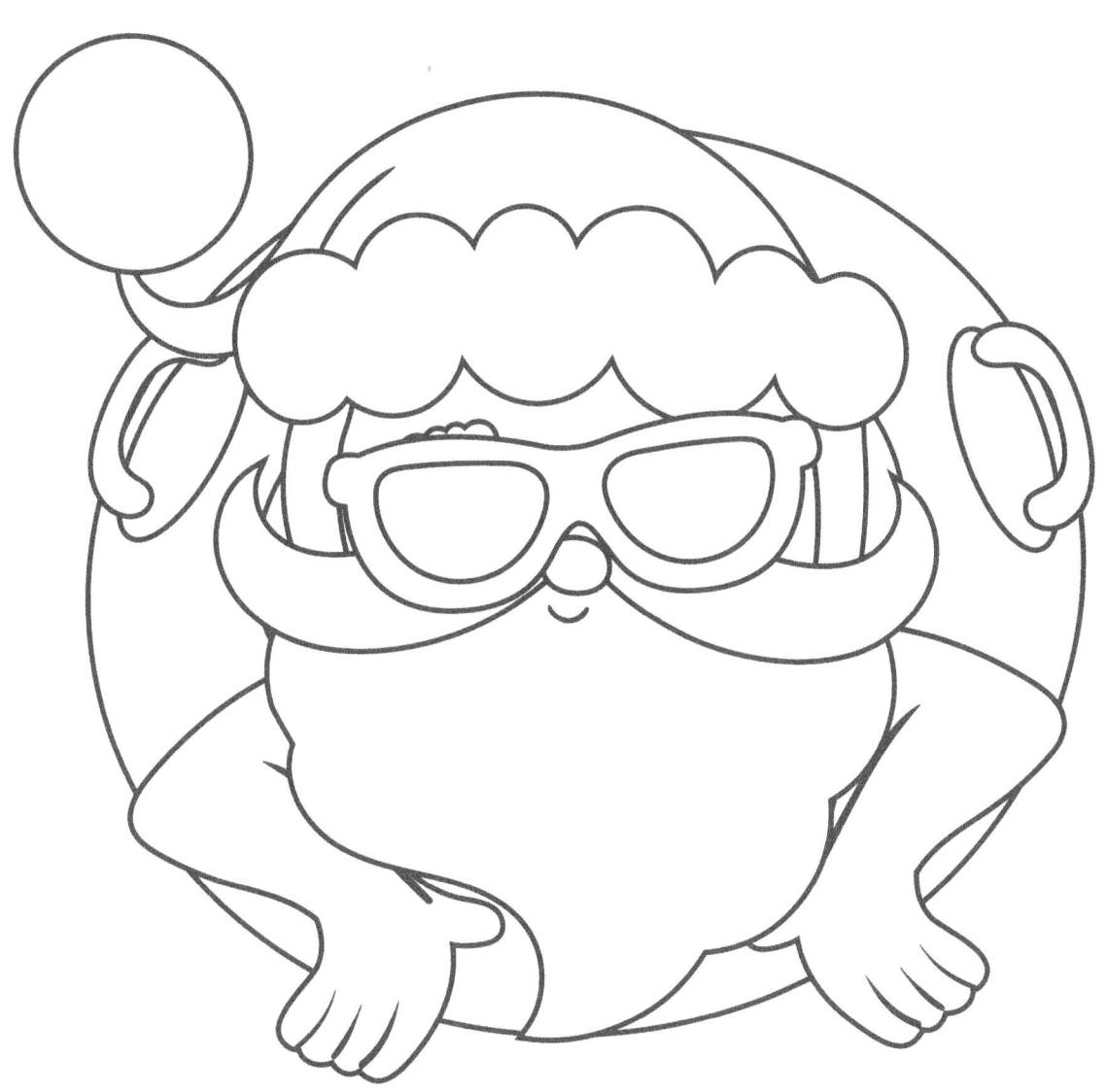

SANTA VACATION

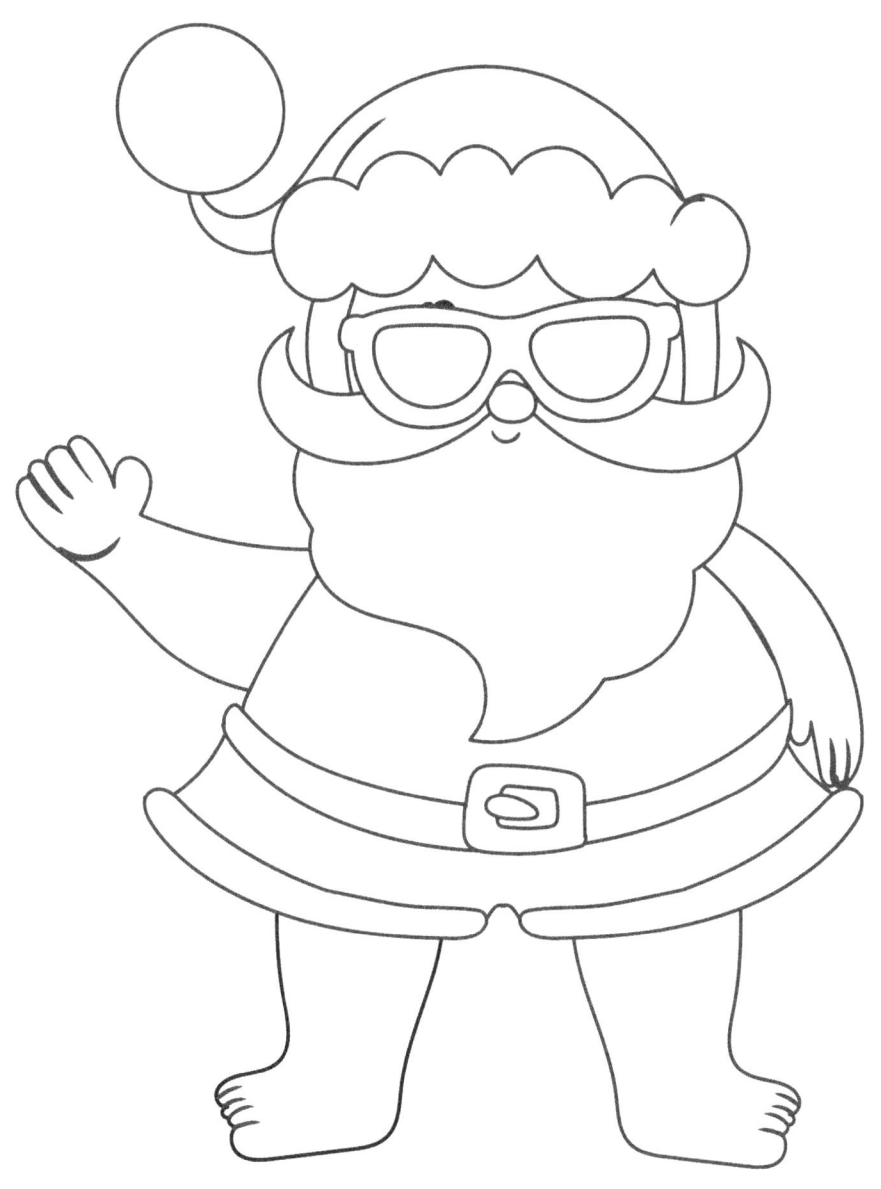

BAKE

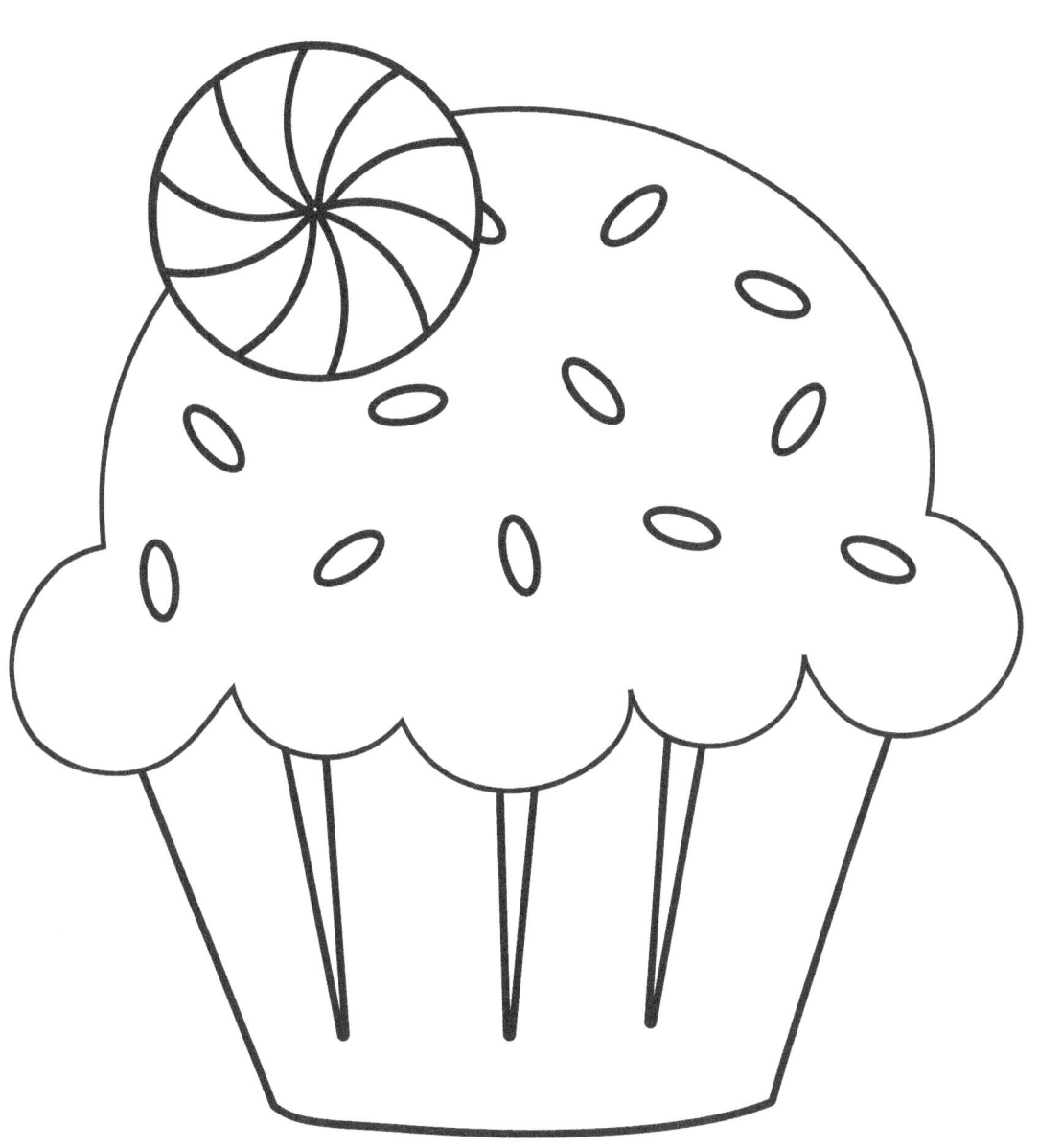

BAKE

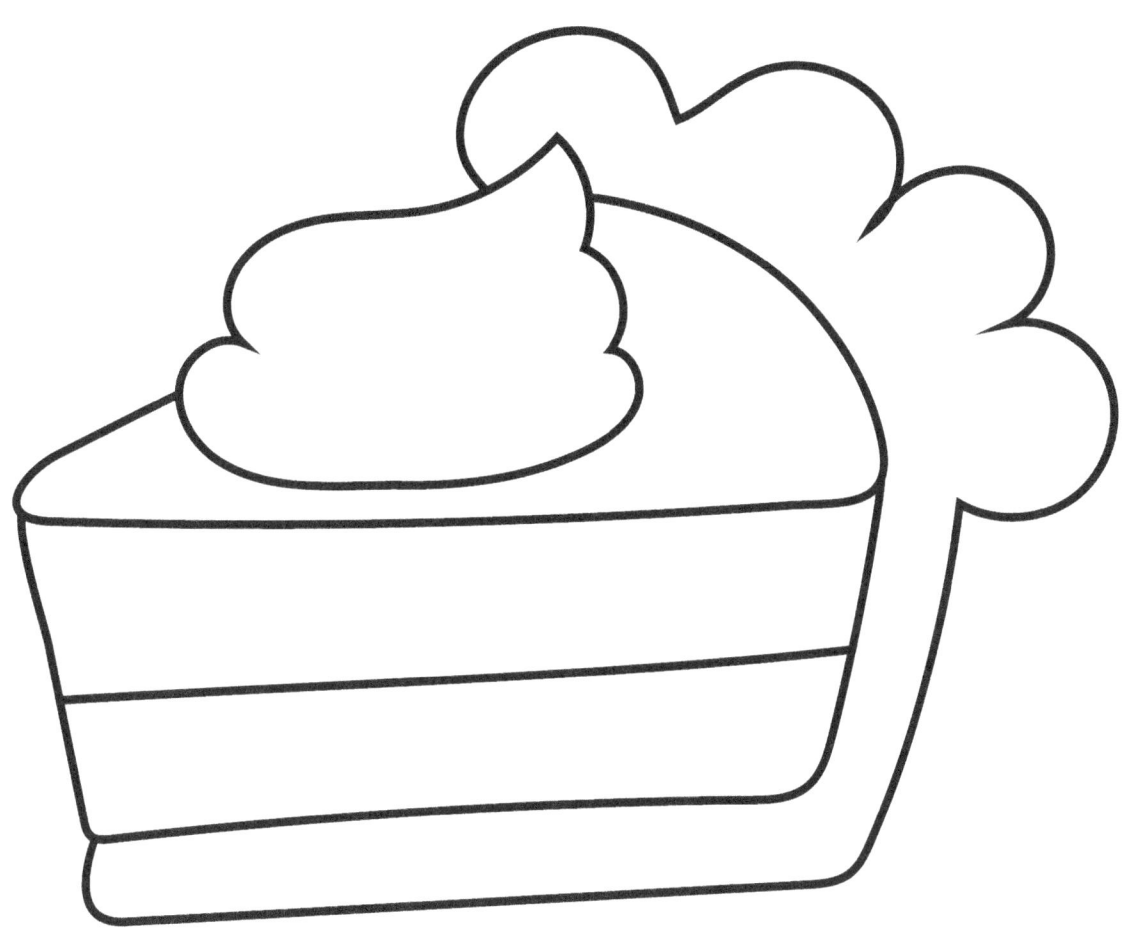

BAKE

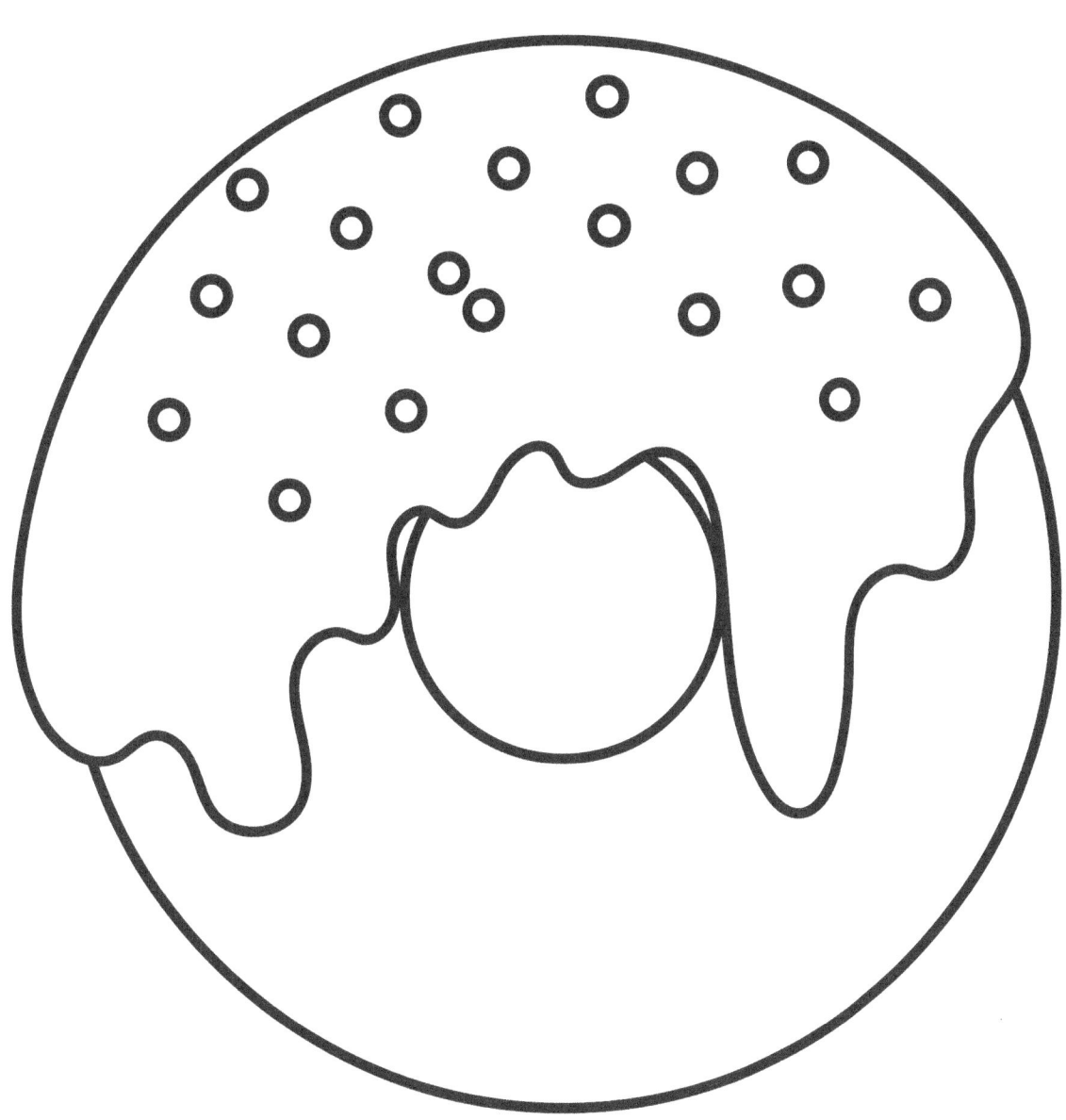

BAKE

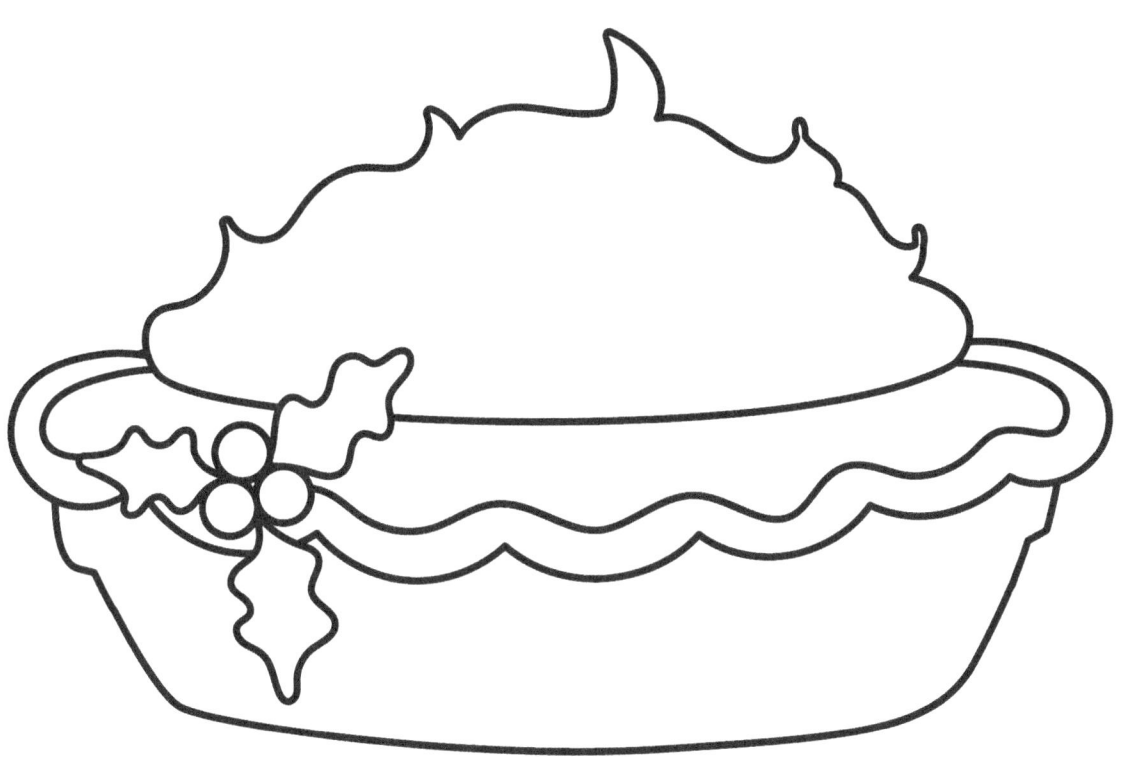

BAKE

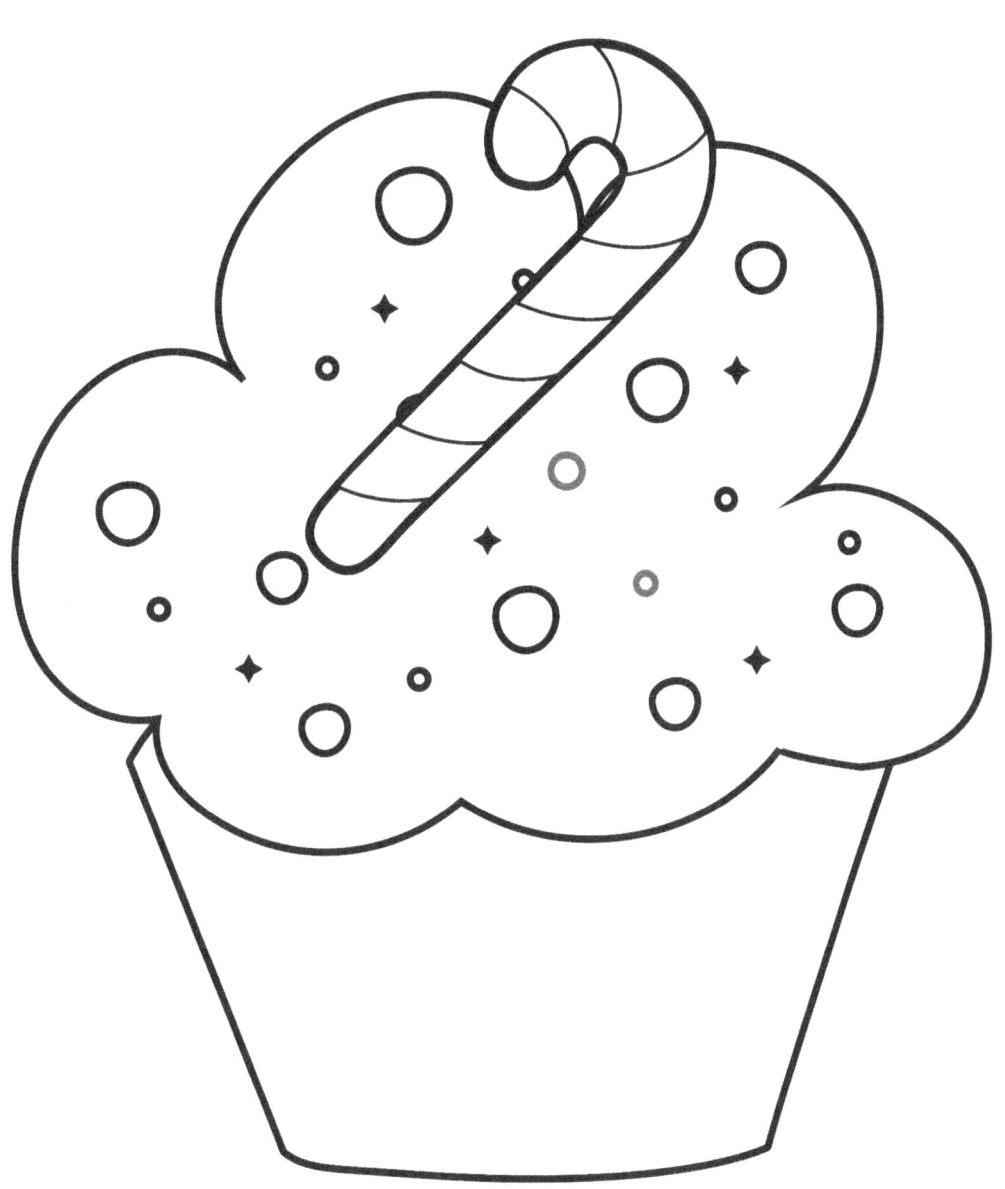

www.ingramcontent.com/pod-product-compliance
Lightning Source LLC
Chambersburg PA
CBHW080838220526
45467CB00008B/2318